Spotsylvania County, Virginia

Order Book Abstracts

1724–1730, Part IV

(1729 – 1730)

Ruth and Sam Sparacio

Heritage Books
2025

HERITAGE BOOKS

AN IMPRINT OF HERITAGE BOOKS, INC.

Books, CDs, and more—Worldwide

For our listing of thousands of titles see our website
at
www.HeritageBooks.com

Published 2025 by
HERITAGE BOOKS, INC.
Publishing Division
5810 Ruatan Street
Berwyn Heights, MD 20740

International Standard Book Number
Paperbound: 978-0-7884-5062-4

SPOTSYLVANIA COUNTY, VIRGINIA
ORDER BOOK
1724-1730 (PART IV)

p.
340

<u>- At a Court held for Spotsylvania County September ye Second Anno Dom: 1729</u>

Present

GOODRICH LIGHTFOOT	JOSEPH BROCK	
WILLIAM SMITH	ROBERT SLATTER	Gentn. Justices
WILLIAM HANSFORD	ROBERT GREEN	

- On petition of JOHN WILKINGS, he is discharged from being Overseer of the Road from WALLERS BRIDGE to EAST NORTH EAST BRIDGE & ordered that JOHN SMITH swrve in his room & that the same tithables which served unto ye said WILKINGS do help the said SMITH cleare & keep in good repair the said Road

- BENJAMIN RUSH, Deputy Sheriff of KING GEORGE COUNTY, made returne of RICHARD BRYANTs &c. Adm. of JONES Execution against THOMAS YATES & WILLIAM HACKNEY for five hundred pounds of tobacco & two hundred ninety five pds Toba: costs

- On motion of Mr. WILLIAM RUSSELL that Mr. HENRY FEILDs Tithables may be added to his gang to help clear ye Road, the same is rejected

- On petition of WILLIAM TAPP, he is discharged from being Overseer of the Road from the COUNTY BRIDGE to NASSANPONAX WHARFE, and ordered that BARTHOLO-MEW WOOD do serve in his room, and that all the tithables that served under the said TAPP do help the said WOOD clear & keep in good repair the said road

- LAWRANCE FRANKLYN acknowledged his Deeds of Lease and Release for land unto THOMAS SALMON at whose motion the same were admitted to record

- THOMAS GAMBRELLs Deeds of Lease and Release for land to JOHN GRAVES were proved by the oaths of THOMAS GRAVES, JOHN GAMBRELL and THOMAS KIMBROW, & att the motion of THOMAS GRAVES in behalf of ye said JOHN GRAVES, the same were admitted to record

- On petition of HENRY FEILD to have his tithables discharged from serveing under GEORGE WHEATLEYs Road & to be added to WILLIAM RUSSELLs gang to help clear his road (being the most convenient) the same is granted

Present ABRAHAM FEILD Gent.

- On Petition of JOHN TALIAFERRO JUNR. that the Road near NICHOLAS CHRISTO-PHERs may extend up to the ROCKEY RUN for the conveniency of the Inhabitants above the same is granted & ordered that Mr. BENJAMIN PORTER & his gang do clear the same

- CHARLES TALIAFERRO acknowledged his Deeds of Lease and Release to FRANCIS CONWAY for land, at whose motion the same were admitted to record

- CHARLES TALIAFERRO acknowledged his Deeds of Lease and Release for land unto HENRY WILLIS and at the motion of PHILEMON CAVENAUGH in behalfe of the said WILLIS, the same are admitted to record

- CHARLES TALIAFERRO acknowledged his Deeds of Lease and Release for land unto WILLIAM MARSHALL; likewise his bond for performance of covenants, & att the motion of the said MARSHALL the same were admitted to record

p.
341

<u>Spotsylvania County Court 2d of September, 1729</u>

- CHARLES TALIAFERRO acknowledged his Deeds of Lease and Release for land unto JAEL JOHNSON and JAMES WILLIAMS, likewise his bond for performance of covenants & att the motion of Mr. MOSLEY BATTALEY in behalfe of the said JAEL and JAMES, the same were admitted to record

- HENRY WILLIS Deeds of Lease and Release unto PHILEMON CAVENAUGH for land were proved by the oaths of WILLIAM MARSHALL, WILLIAM STROTHER and WILLIAM CAVE & att the motion of the said CAVENAUGH the same were admitted to record

- On petition of HENRY WILLIS & PHILLEMON CAVENAUGH in behalfe of themselves & others to have a Road from the said WILLIS's MILL to the COURT HOUSE over MUDDY RUN is rejected

- On petition of WILLIAM DAVIS, JAMES MACK CULLOUGH &c. to have an Overseer appointed in the Room of JOHN LEE who is gone out of the County of the Road commonly called the COUNTY MOUNTAIN ROAD for the use of their Plantations to goe unto the said MOUNTAIN ROAD is granted, & ordered that JAMES MACK CULLOUGH be Overseer thereof & that the said Petitioners, WILLIAM DAVIS, JAMES McCULLOUGH, DENNIS LINDSEY & GEORGE WOOTEN (name partially blurred) with WILLIAM McCONICOs & RICHARD SHARPs tithables (where ye SHARP now lives) to help him clear the same

- JOHN TALIAFERRO Gentn. exhibited an additional Inventory of ROBERT TALIAFERROs Estate as came to his hands since as Executor of the said ROBERT which was ordered to be recorded

- In the action of Trespass upon the Case brought p JAMES TAYLOR Gentn. against THOMAS CHEW and LARKING CHEW, Admrs. with the Will annexed of LARKING CHEW deced. the same is continued to the next Court

- In the action of Debt brought p JERIMIAH BRONAUGH JUNR. & ROSE his Wife, Admrs. &c. of JOHN DINWIDDIE deced vs: ABRAHAM FEILD, the same is continued at the Plantifes cost

- On the Scire facias brought p ALEXANDER MACKFARLAND vs. THOMAS CHEW & LARKIN CHEW, Admrs. &c. of LARKING CHEW deced, the Defendants suffered Judgment to pass against the said CHEWs Estate in the hands of the said Administrators for thirteen hundred and eight five pounds of tobacco with costs; It is therefore ordered that the said Administrators (with ye Will annexed) do pay to the said Plantife the same out of the said LARKIN CHEW deced Estate with costs alias Exo.

- In the action of Debt brought p GEORGE BRAXTON Gentn. Plt. against THOMAS CHEW & LARKIN CHEW,. Admrs. with the Will annexed of LARKIN CHEW deced, Defendts., Judgment passed for ten pounds Eleven shillings & eleven pence Sterling and five pounds five shillings & eleven pence currt. money with costs against the said LARKIN CHEW deced Estate in the hands of the said Administrators; It is therefore ordered that the said Admrs. do pay to the said Plantife the same out of the said LARKIN CHEW deced Estate alias Exo.

- On the Scire facias brought p ANN JAMES, Admx. &c. of EDWARD SOUTHALL deced; against THOMAS CHEW & LARKIN CHEW, Admrs. with the Will annexed of LARKIN CHEW deced; Judgment passed for two punds sixteen shillings & three pence Sterlin and two hundred & seventy three pounds of tobacco with costs against ye sd LARKIN CHEW Estate (deced) in the hands of the said Administrators; It is therefore ordered that the said Administrators do pay unto the said Plantife the same out of the said LARKIN CHEW deced Estate with costs alias Exo.

p.   Spotsylvania County Court, 2d of September 1729
342   - In the action of Trespass upon the Case between WILLIAM BARTLETT & WIL-
        LIAM BARTLETT, Ass: of SAMUELL BARTLETT, Plt. against HARRY BEVERLEY
Gentn. Defendt., oyer is granted the Defendt.

- On the Attachment obtained p WILLIAM RUSSELL against the Estate of EDWARD WINGFIELD. the same is continued to the next Court

- On the Attachment obtained p JOHN DOWDE against the Estate of RICHARD

LEWIS for fiveteen pounds of tobacco, the same being served in the hands of JAMES HORSNAIL & FRANCIS MICHAEL, Ordered that the Sheriff do summons the sd HORSNAIL & MICHAEL to appear and give an Accot: to the next Court what of the said LEWIS Estate they had in their hands when ye said Attachment was served

    - In the action of Trespass upon the Case brought p THOMAS BENSON Plt. agt. JOSEPH SMITH Gentn. Defendant for fifty pounds current money damage, issue being joyned & put to a Jury for tryall p name LARKIN CHEW &c. who after being sworn & heard all evedences &c. brought in their verdict Vizt. Wee of the Jury find for the Plantife twelve pounds currant money, LARKIN CHEW, foreman, which verdict at the Plantifes motion was admitted to record, the Defendt. afterwards craved liberty & assighn Errors in arrest of Judgment which were admitted & received & ordered that thay be referred to the next Court for arguement

    - In the action of Trespass upon the Case between JAMES TAYLOR Gent. Plt. and EDWARD WATTS Deft., for twelve hundred pounds of tobacco damage, the Defendt. appeared & confessed Judgment for One thousand pounds of tobacco and Ten Shillings current money with costs & an attorneys fee; It is therefore ordered that the sd WATTS do pay the sd TAYLOR the same with costs & an attorneys fee alias Execution

    - JOHN FOSTER, Deputy Sheriff, made return of the following Executions Vizt. JAMES HORSNAIL Exo. vs JOHN CAMPELL for L 5...7...5 Currt. money & 3271 1/2 lbs. Tobo. costs·

    - On petition of ABRAM FIELD Gent. to have a Dedimus Potestatem issue for the taking of NATHANIEL GRAYs Evedence of WESTMORELAND COUNTY (he being very ancient & unable to attend this Court) being the materiall Evedence for him in ye Tryall depending between him & JERIMIAH BRONAUGH JUNR. & ROSE his Wife, Admrs. with the Will annexed of JOHN DINWIDDIE deced, the same is granted & ordered that the Clerk do issue and direct one to BIRDINE ASHTON and JOHN ELLIOTT Gentn. to examine ye said GRAY (giving the Plantiff notice) and for them to make report thereof to the next Court

    - Present THOMAS CHEW Gent.

    - Majr. GOODRICH LIGHTFOOT, Capt. ROBT. SLAUGHTER and his Officers, FRANCIS KIRKLEY & WILLIAM PAYTON, Capt. JOHN SCOTT and his Officers, JOSEPH HAWKINS & JOHN LIGHTFOOT, Capt. WILLIAM BLEDSOE & his Officers, JAMES WILLIAMS & GEORGE HOME, came into Court & took the Oath & signed the Test &c. as the Law directs which was administred to them p JOSEPH BROCK & ABRAM FIELD Gentlemen

    - On the complaint made by EDWIN HICKMAN Gent., Sheriff against DAVID JONES for not aiding and assisting his Deputy Sheriff to retake EDWARD WINGFIELD who broke out of Prison, the Court having heard all evedence & arguements on each side are of oppinion that the Sheriffs Complaint is good and that the sd JONES be fined Five Shillings current money or fifty pounds of tobacco to our Sovereign Lord the King for his contempt and pay costs

    - In the action of the Case between JERIMIAH MURDOCK Gent. and JONAS JENKINS Defendt. the said Plantiff joyned ye Defts. plea and ye tryall thereof is referred to ye next Court

p.   Spotsylvania County Court 2d of September 1729
343   - On the Attachment obtained p MARY HAWKINS, Widow, against THOMAS TYLERs Estate the same is postponed till to Morrow

    - In the action of Debt between WILLIAM STROTHER Gent. Plt. and THOMAS BURN Defendt., the said Defendt. put in his demurrer which ye Plt. joyned and referred to the next Court for Arguement

    - In the action of Trespass upon ye Case between Ditto and Ditto the same order

- WILLIAM RUSSELL, Admr. with the Will annexed of WILLIAM THOMPSON deced, returned an Inventory & appraisment of ye sd Deced Estate which was ordered to be recorded

- On the Attachment obtained by WILLIAM RUSSELL against the Estate of JOHN BLACKLEY for seven pounds ten Shillings current money due p Accot: having proved ye same on Oath, Judgment is granted him for the same with costs & an attorneys fee and THOMAS BYRN delivering into Court an Obligation of WILLIAM BLEDSOE Gentn. payable to ye Defendt. (that he lodged in his hands) for Six hundred pounds of tobacco, which the said BLEDSOE had no discount against, Therefore ordered that the said Tobacco be sold p the Sheriff as the Law directs to satisfie the above Judgment so farr as it will amount to and make return thereof to the next Court

- On the petition of WILLIAM RUSSELL, Admr. with the Will annexed of WILLIAM THOMPSON deced, agst. GOODRICH LIGHTFOOT Gent. for Cattle &c. the same is continued by consent

- In the action of Trespass between JOSEPH SMITH Gent. Plt. and THOMAS BENSON Defendt., the said Defendt. put in his plea which the Plt. joyned and referred to the next Court for tryall

- On motion of JOHN SCOTT Gent. to have the MOUNTAIN ROAD devided from Capt. THOMAS CHEW MILL to the COUNTY LINE is granted and ordered that JOHN MINOR be Overseer thereof & that all the tithables from above THOMAS BEALs Quarter do help the said MINOR to clear & keep the same in good repair

- Ordered that the Court be adjourned till to Morrow morning eight of the Clock

- At a Court continued & held for Spotsylvania County September the third Anno Dom. 1729   Present

THOMAS CHEW	JOSEPH BROCK	
WILLIAM BLEDSOE	ABRAM FIELD	Gentlemen Justices

- In the action of Debt between RICHARD LONG, Ass: of JOHN SUTTON, Plt. and WILLIAM RUSSELL Defendt., ye sd Defendt. put in a plea which ye Plt. joyned & referred to the next Court for tryall

- In the action of the Case between RICHARD LONG Plt. and WILLIAM HUTCHESON Defendt. ye sd Defendt. craved leave to plead divers matters which is granted, afterwards put in a plea which ye Plt. joyned and the tryall thereof is referred to the next Court

Present WM. HANSFORD, Gent.

- In the action of Trespass upon ye Case between WILLIAM CUDDING Plt. and JOSEPH ROBERTS Defendt., for thirty pounds current money, the same being agreed, ordered that ye sd suit be dismist

p. Spotsylvania County Court 3d of September 1729
344 - On the Attachment obtained p CHARLES CHISWELL Gent. against the Estate of THOMAS TYLER for seventeen pounds one Shilling & one farthing current money due p Accot: which being proved, Judgment is granted him for the same with costs and an attorneys fee; EDWIN HICKMAN Sheriff according to summonds appeared and declared that he had in his hands (remaining of the Negroe as was sold as p Accot: given in), twelve pounds & seven pence currant money and ANDREW HARRISON appeared according to summonds and on oath declared that he had fourteen hundred pounds of tobacco in his hands (which p Consent with ye Court & ye Plantiff) was stated at 12/6 p cent amounts to Eight pounds fiveteen Shillings; Ordered that ye sd EDWIN

HICKMAN & ANDREW HARRISON pay the same to the said CHISWELL to satisife ye sd Judgment and costs ass farr as it ammounts unto

- In the action of Trespass and assault between CHRISTOPHER WATTERS Plt. and JOHN KILGORE Defendt., for fifty pounds damage, the Plantiff failing to appear and prosecute his suit, on motion of ye sd Defendt., the same is ordered to be dismist with costs and an attorneys fee; It is therefore ordered that ye sd Plt. do pay unto the said Defendt. his costs & an attorneys fee alias Exo.

- On the Injunction in Chancery between ROBERT SPOTSWOOD and THOMAS DAVIS the Defendt. put in a demurrer and time given the Complt. to consider the same

- On the petition of SUSANNAH LIVINGSTON, Admx. of WM. LIVINGSTON deced, agst. GEORGE HOME, the same is postponed

- In the action of Trespass upon the Case between RICHARD LOVILE Plt. and GEORGE WOODROOF Defendt., the same being agreed, ordered that the same be dismist

- In the action of Trespass upon the Case between JOSEPH ROBERTS Plt. and THOMAS ALLEN Defendt., on ye sd Defendts. motion oyer is granted him

- In the action of Debt between THOMAS CHEW, Ass: of PAYTON SMITH, Plt., and CHARLES CURTIS & DAVID KINKED Defendts., the same being agreed, ordered that ye sd Suit be dismist

- In the action of Trespass upon the Case between JOHN SNELL Plt. and WILLIAM FRAZIER Defendt., the said Defendt. failing to appear and answer when called, on ye Plts. motion an order against the sd Deft. and his security is granted him

- ROBERT SPOTSWOOD came into open Court and make oath to his account against JOHN SIMSON which was ordered to be certified

- On the petition of EDWARD FRANKLYN about altering the Road from Capt. JERIMIAH CLOWDERs ROAD to MATTAPONY CHURCH, the said petition is ordered to be dismist

- Ordered that EDWARD FRANKLYN be Overseer of the Road from Capt. JERIMIAH CLOWDERs ROAD to MATTAPONY CHURCH along the Ridge ye nearest and best way to the said CHURCH and that all the tithables that served under him before do help him clear the same

- Absent THOMAS CHEW, Gent.

- On the petition of THOMAS LARKIN Gent. of ANN ARUNDLL: County in ye Province of MARYLAND against THOMAS CHEW and LARKIN CHEW, Admrs. &c. with the Will annexed of LARKIN CHEW deced for Seventy nine pounds three shillings and one farthing Sterling & nineteen pounds six Shillings & six pence Current money the same being due p Accot: which was proved by Oath, the Defendts. came into Court and suffered Judgment to pass for the same with costs with a release of Errors against ye sd LARKIN CHEW deced Estate in ye hands of ye sd THOMAS CHEW & LARKIN CHEW, Admrs. &c. of the Will annexed of ye sd LARKIN CHEW deced; It is therefore ordered that the said Admrs. do pay the sd LARKIN ye same out of ye sd CHEW deced Estate in ye sd Admrs. &c. hands with costs alias Execution

p.   Spotsylvania County Court 3d of September 1729
343   - Present THOMAS CHEW, Gent and JOHN SCOTT
- On motion of EDWARD FRANKLYN, Mr. ROBERT BAYLORs tithables at his Quarter THOMAS CREDERS & JOSEPH ROBERTS are ordered to be added to his gang

- On the action of Trespass upon the Case between MARY HAWKINS & JOSEPH HAWKINS, Admrs. of JOHN HAWKINS deced, Plts. and CHARLES GOODALL Defendt. special bail being required is granted, Mr. ZACHARY LEWIS entered himself special bail for ye sd Defendt who afterward put in a plea & on ye Plts. motion time granted them to consider the same

- On the petition of JOHN HEWS against WILLIAM RUSSELL, Admr. with the Will annexed of WILLIAM THOMPSON deced, for six hundred & forty nine pounds of tobacco due p Bill, the same being proved by oath, the Defendt. appeared and suffered Judgment to pass against the said THOMPSON deced Estate in the hands of the said Admr. &c. with costs; It is therefore ordered that the said RUSSELL, Admr. &c. of THOMPSON deced, do pay the sd HEWS the same out of ye sd Deced Estate in the hands of ye sd Admr. &c. with costs alias Execution

- On the Attachment obtained by MARY HAWKINS, Widow, against ye Estate of THOMAS TYLER for Six hundred pounds of tobacco and fourteen Shillings & six pence current money due by Accot: which ye Plt. proved on oath, Judgment is granted for the same with costs & an attorneys fee. NICHOLAS CHRISTOPHER appeared according to summonds and on oath declared that he had one Coat & Jacket of Drugett about half worn, one small frying pan, one Storking Ax, two shewmakers knives, one hand saw, one old Blankett & one Cow bell & ye Corn that is in ye sd TYLERs House & his papers, And THOMAS YATES appeared according to summonds & on oath declared that he had passed a Bill to ye sd TYLER & also had a discount against it, but could not tell the ballance due to ye sd TYLER, & JOHN CHRISTOPHER came into Court and on oath declared that he had THOMAS YATES Bill to THOMAS TYLER in his possession; Ordered that the Sheriff sell the above things which are in the hands of NICHOLAS CHRISTOPHER And that the Attachment be continued to the next Court for YATES to draw up his discount, And that the Sheriff do take the sd YATES's Bill and make return of his proceedings to the next Court

- On the petition of SUSANNAH LIVINGSTON, Admx. of WILLIAM LIVINGSTON deced, agst. GEORGE HOME for one pound nineteen shillings & four pence current money or three hundred and Ninty four pounds of tobacco due p Accot: the Defendts. plea being joyned and put to ye Court for tryall, who after hearing all arguements and the Defendts. Oath to his discount, are of oppinion that Judgment pass for three hundred & fourteen pounds of tobacco with costs & an attorneys fee agst. ye sd Defendt., It is therefore ordered that the sd Defendt. do pay the sd Plt. the same with costs and an attorneys fee alias execution

- On petition of ZACHARY LEWIS against WILLIAM RUSSELL, Admr. with the Will annexed of WM. THOMPSON deced, for fifty Shillings current money due by Accot:, the Plt. having proved the same by Oath, the Defendt. appeared & suffered Judgment to pass against ye sd THOMPSON deced Estate in ye hands of ye sd WM. RUSSELL, Admr. &c. for the same with costs; It is therefore ordered that the said Admr. &c. do pay the same out of ye sd THOMPSONs deced Estate in the hands of ye sd Admr. &c. with costs alias Execution

- In ye action of Debt between GEORGE PROCTOR Plt. and JOHN YOUNG Defendt., the Attachment being returned not served on anything by the Sheriff, on the Plts. motion the same continued to the next Court

- In ye action of Trespass upon ye Case between JOHN WALLER Plt. and EDWARD WINGFIELD Deft., the same is continued to the next Court

p.   Spotsylvania County Court 3d of September 1729
346   - On the Summonds in Chancery between ROBERT SPOTSWOOD and THOMAS DAVIS
It is ordered that the Clerk do file the Summonds with the Injunction that was first filed

- In the action of Debt between Collo. ALEXANDER SPOTSWOOD Plt. and ANDREW GLASPE Defendt. for one pounds sixteen shillings & two pence half penny Currt. money (special bail being required is granted) afterwards the Defendt. in Custody of EDWIN

HICKMAN Gent. Sheriff appeared and confessed Judgment for the same with costs & an attorneys fee; It is therefore ordered that the said Defendt. in custody as aforesaid do pay unto ye sd Plt. the same with costs & an attorneys fee alias Execution

    - In the action of Debt between JONATHAN HOOD Plt. and ALEXANDER SPOTSWOOD Esqr. Defendt., the Plt. put in a demurrer and on motion of the Defendt. time is granted him to consider the same

    - In the action of Debt between REUBEN WELSH Gent. Plt. and DANIEL BROWNE Defendt., for six pounds two Shillings & eleven pence current money due by Bill, the Plt. being dead, ordered that the said suit be dismist

    - In the action of Trespass upon the Case between THOMAS BENSON Plt. and JOSEPH SMITH Defendt., issue joyned & referred for tryall

    - In the action of the Case between JOHN TALIAFERRO Gent. Plt. and WILLIAM BICKHAM Defendt., further oyer is granted him ye sd Defendt.

    - On the petition of ANN QUARLES, Widow of JOHN QUARLES deced, in behalf of herself and JOHN QUARLES, her Son, an Infant, foran acre of land on NASSANPONAX RUN to build a MILL &c., the same being referred to be valued and their report being not returned, Likewise the said Petitioners failing to appear and answer the same, ordered that the sd Petition be dismist

    - In the action of the Case between BENJAMIN GRAYSON by his next Friend, JOHN GRAYSON, Plt. and HARRY BEVERLEY Defendt., the same is continued at the sd Defendts. costs

    - In the action of Debt between WILLIAM STROTHER Plt. and JOHN HEWS Defendt. the Sheriff having returned a Copy Left on the plurias capias, at ye Plts. motion ye same is continued

    - JOHN PIGG failing to appear when called to answer the Presentment of the Grand Jury for breaking out & burning of ye COUNTY PRISON, the Kings Attorney refuseing to prosecute the presentment any further p reason ye said PIGG did not appear according to bond & security he gave the Sheriff, ordered that the same be dismist

    - On petition of GEORGE HOME against EDWARD PRICE Defendt., for five hundred & fifty pounds of tobacco due by Accot: and the sd Plt. proving ye same on oath, the Court are of oppinion that Judgmt. should pass for the same & with costs and an attorneys fee for the non appearance of ye sd Defendt., It is therefore ordered that ye sd Defendt. do pay unto ye sd Plantiff the same with costs & an attorneys fee alias Execution

    - In the action of Debt between GEORGE TILLY Plt. and WILLIAM PERRY Defendt. for one pound eleven shillings & six pence current money due by Bill, the said Defendt. failing to appear and answer when called, on the Plts. motion an Attachment is granted him

p.   Spotsylvania County Court. 3d of September 1729
347   - In the action of Trespass upon the Case between GEORGE TILLY Plt. and JAMES DYER Defendt., for ten pounds current money damage, the same being agreed, ordered that ye sd suit be dismist

    - In the action of the Case between RICHARD CHEEK Plt. and DENNIS MORGAIN Defendt., for four hundred & twenty five pounds of tobacco due by Accot: there being no prosecution of either party, ordered that the same be dismist

    - In the action of Trespass between JAMES McCOLLOUGH Plt. and EDWIN HICKMAN Gent. Sheriff Defendt., the said Defendt. put in a plea & demurrer, And ordered to be continued p reason of JOHN MERCER, the Plantiffs Attorney, being absent

    - In the action of Detinue between GEORGE NIX Plt. and EDWARD PRICE Defendt., the Defendt. failing to appear and answer ye same when called, an order is granted against him ye sd Defendt. and Sheriff

- In the action of Trespass upon ye Case between WILLIAM CUDDING Plt. and JOSEPH ROBERTS Defendt., for fifty pounds Sterling damage, the said suit being agreed, ordered that the same be dismist

- On the petition of GEORGE HOME against MICHAEL HOLT for five hundred & fifty pounds of tobacco due by Bill; the Plt. having proved ye same by Oath, And the said Defendt. failing to appear according to summonds and answer the same, the Court are of oppinion that Judgment should pass for the same with costs and an attorneys fee against the sd Defendt., It is therefore ordered that the said HOLT do pay unto the said HOME the same with costs and an attorneys fee alias Execution

- On the Attachment obtained by WILLIAM RUSSELL, Admr. with the Will annexed of WILLIAM THOMPSON deced, against DENNIS MORGAINs Estate for seven hundred and seventy five pounds of tobacco, the Sheriff having made return served in the hands of JOHN CARDER, JAMES MORGAIN and WILLIAM RICHESON, On ye Plts. motion it is ordered that ye sd CARDER, MORGAIN and RICHESON be summoned to the next Court to declare what of ye sd DENNIS MORGAINs Estate they had in their hands when ye sd Attachment was served on them

- In the action of Debt between GEORGE HOME Plt. and WILLIAM RUSSELL Defendt the same on ye sd Defendts. motion is continued at his costs

- In the action of the Case between JOHN WIGLESWORTH Plt. and HENRY GOODLOE Gent. Defendt., the same is postponed

- In the action of Trespass upon ye Case between JOSEPH SMITH Gent. Plt. and WILLIAM RUSSELL Defendt., the Plantiff joyned ye Defendts. plea and the tryall thereof is referred to the next Court

- In the action of Trespass upon the Case between JAMES JONES Plt. and EDWARD WINGFIELD Defendt., the same is continued till next Court

- In the action of Trespass upon ye Case between WILLIAM WOODFORD Gent. Plt. and JOHN TALIAFERRO Gent., Exr. &c. of ROBERT TALIAFERRO deced, Deft., the same is continued till next Court

- In the action of Debt between ALEXANDER McFARLAND Plt. and THOMAS CHEW and LARKIN CHEW, Admrs. with the Will annexed of LARKIN CHEW Gent. late Sheriff deced, Defendts., the Defendts. put in a plea and demurrer and on the Plantiffs motion time is granted him to consider the same

      - Present GOODRICH LIGHTFOOT, Gentn.

p. Spotsylvania County Court 3d of September 1729
348   - On the petition of CHARLES CHISWELL Gent. & Partners &c. for BRIDGES to be built over the RIVERS &c. at ye County Charge, the Gentlemen appointed by the last Courts order not fully comply'd with ye same, Ordered that the said order be continued for the sd Gentlemen to compleat the same, and make report of their proceedings to the next Court

- On motion of Mr. JOHN CHEW, he is allowed for five days attendance as he was summoned an evedence for THOMAS BENSON against JOSEPH SMITH Gent (he haveing sworn to the time) It is therefore ordered that the said BENSON do pay to ye sd CHEW the same with costs alias Execution

      - JOHN FOSTER the same order granted for SMITH against BENSON
      - ANTHONY FOSTER the same order granted for Ditto ads. Ditto
      - NICHOLAS HAWKINS the same order granted for Ditto ads. Ditto
      - On petition of BENJAMIN CAVE, he is discharged from being Overseer of the

Road from GERMANNA to the MARKED STONES, and Ordered that JOHN GORDEN do serve in his room, and that the same Tithables which served under the said CAVE do help the said GORDEN clear and keep in good repair the said Road

- In the action of Debt between ALEXANDER SPOTSWOOD Esqr. Plt. and ANDREW HARRISON Defendt., on ye sd Defendts. motion the same is continued at his costs

- In the action of Trespass upon ye Case between BENJAMIN GRAYSON p JOHN GRAYSON his next Friend, Plt. and CHRISTOPHER WATTERS Defendt., the same is continued to the next Court

- On motion of Mr. EDMUND BAGG, he is allowed for two days attendance and for comeing and going seventy miles as he was summoned an evedence for ALEXANDER SPOTSWOOD Esqr. against ANDREW HARRISON; It is therefore ordered that the said SPOTSWOOD do pay the said BAGG the same with costs alias Exo.

- Mr. BENJAMIN WINSLOW, the same order granted for Ditto agst. Ditto

- JAMES KENNY the same order granted and for twenty eight miles comeing & going with his ferriages for Ditto against Ditto

- On motion of ANDREW HARRISON to have a Dedimus Potestatem issue for the taking of JOHN KENNYs, SARAH KENNEYs, JAMES CANNEY JUNR. evedence of KING GEORGE COUNTY (they being sick and unable to attend the Court) being materiall evedences for him in the Tryall depending between him and ALEXANDER SPOTSWOOD Esqr. the same is granted, And Ordered that the Clerk do issue and direct one to WILLIAM THORNTON and WILLIAM STROTHER Gentlemen to examine the said JOHN, SARAH and JAMES (giving the Plt. or his Attorney notice) and for them to make report thereof to the next Court

- On petition of BENJAMIN CAVE for & in behalf of himself and others for a Road from the WALNUT BRANCH on ye North side ye RAPPADAN down the Ridge & to cross ye RAPPADAN so down to the SOUTH WEST MOUNTAIN CHAPPELL is granted and Ordered that the said BENJAMIN CAVE be Overseer thereof, And that all the Tithables which are scituate adjacent on ye River do help him ye sd CAVE clear the same

- In the action of Debt between WILLIAM ALLEN Plt. and GOODRICH LIGHTFOOT Gent., late Sheriff, Defendt., for four pounds current money and one hundred and eight pounds of tobacco due by Judgment, An Order last Court being comfirmed for what should appear due this p Writ of Enquiry against ye sd Defendt., & EDWIN HICKMAN Gent. Sheriff. And a Jury being Impannelled and sworn p name LARKIN CHEW &c. who after having heard all arguements and the Defendts. discount, which ye sd Plt. allowed, retired, & brought in their verdict Vizt. We of the Jury find for the Plantiff two pounds five shillings & five pence Currt. money and one hundred & eight pounds of tobacco for Debt and Damage fourteen shillings & eleven pence for detaining the said Debt, LARKIN CHEW foreman.

p.   Spotsylvania County Court 3d of September 1729
349   which Verdict at ye Plts. motion was admitted to record and Judgment granted
        for the same with costs & an attorneys fee; It is therefore ordered that the said
Defendt. & Sheriff do pay unto ye sd Plt. the same alias Exo.

- On the petition of JOHN ROBINSON against WILLIAM RUSSELL, Admr. &c. with the Will annexed of WM. THOMPSON deced, for two pounds five shillings & three pence current money due by Accot., which was proved on Oath, the Defendt. suffered Judgment to pass for the same with costs (when assets when the Debts of greater Dignity are fully paid and satisfied) against the said THOMPSONs deced Estate in ye hands of ye sd Administrator &c.

- In the action of Trespass upon the Case between GEORGE HOME Plt. and

CHARLES DUETT JUNR. Defendt., Judgment by Nihil Dicit is granted

- In the action of the Case between WILLIAM SMITH Gent. Plt. and EDWARD WINGFIELD Defendt., an order having passed against ye sd Defendt. in Custody of ye Sheriff last Court for the sd Defendts. non appearance and he now failing to appear and answer when called, the said Order is confirmed for what shall appear due p Writ of Enquiry next Court

- In the action of Debt between CHARLES BURGES Plt. and OWEN HUMPHRYS Defendt., the Sheriff having returned a Copy Left and ye Defendt. failing to appear & answer, on ye Plts. motion a plurias capias is granted him

- In the action of Debt between JOHN SMITH Plt. and GEORGE HOME and WILLIAM MOORE Defendts., the said Defendts. put in a plea and time given ye Plt. to consider the same

- WILLIAM SMITH Gent. came into Court and made oath that two pounds fourteen Shillings & eleven pence current money was due of this Accot: of EDWARD WINGFIELD to him which was ordered to be certified

- In the action of Debt between JOHN SMITH Plt. and WILLIAM RUSSELL Defendt., the said Defendt. put in a plea which ye Plt. joyned and tryal referred to the next Court

- Ditto vs WILLIAM MOORE, Defendt. put in a plea & time given the Plt. to consider ye same

- In the action of Debt between JAMES BOOTH Plt. and ISAAC MAYFIELD Defendt., special bail being required last Court was granted, ABRAM MAYFIELD & WILLIAM BICKHAM came into Court & entered themselves Special Bail for ye sd Defendt., who afterwards put in a plea which was joyned and the tryall thereof is referred to the next Court

- In the action of Debt between JOSEPH FOX Plt. and GOODRICH LIGHTFOOT Gent., late Sheriff, Defendt., the said Defendt. put in a plea which was joyned & the tryall thereof is referred to the next Court

- In ye action of Debt between LYONEL LYDE of City of BRISTOL, Mercht., Plt. and JOHN TALIAFERRO Gent., Exr. of ROBERT TALIAFERRO deced, the same is ordered to be continued

- In the action of Trespass upon the Case between JAMES HORSNAIL Plt. and DENNIS MORGAIN Defendt., for ten pounds current money damage, the Attachment being returned p the Sheriff nothing to be found in my Bailiwick, Ordered that the suit be dismist

- In the action of Debt between PHILIP SMITH and COMPANY, Merchts., in LONDON Plts. and CHRISTOPHER WATTERS Defendt., for five pounds nineteen shillings and three pence Sterling money of England due by a Protested Bill of Exchange &c., An order having last Court passed against the sd Defendt. and HENRY CAMMELL his Security for the non appearance of ye sd Defendt., and he now failing to appear when called & answer the same, the said Order is confirmed against ye sd Defendt. & his security for the same with costs & an attorneys fee; It is therefore ordered that ye sd Defendt. & his security do pay the sd Plt. the same with costs & an attorneys fee alias Execution

p.   Spotsylvania County Court 3d of September 1729
350   - Ordered that the COUNTY LEVY be laid next Court and that the Sheriff do give
         Publick Notice accordingly

- In the action of Trespass upon the Case between WILLIAM RUSSELL, Admr. &c. with the Will annexed of WILLIAM THOMPSON deced, Plt. and ANDREW GLASPE Defendt., the said Defent. moved that Veiwers might be appointed to veiw and value the work done on ye Dwelling House by the said THOMPSON deced is granted And Ordered that

ROBERT GREEN Gent.and FRANCIS MICHALL do value the same and make return of their proceedings to the next Court, And that Judgment should pass according to ye sd Veiwers return

- In the action of Debt between JAMES TAYLOR Gent. and GEORGE DOWDEY Defendt., the same is continued to the next Court

- In the action of Debt between JOHN ROBINSON Plt. and ANDREW GLASPE Defendt., for five hundred and fifty pounds of tobacco, cask and conveniency due by Bill, the sd Defendt. appeared and confessed Judgment for the same with costs & an attorneys fee; It is therefore ordered that the Defendt. do pay unto the sd Plantiff the same with costs & an attorneys fee alias Exo.

- In the action of Trespass upon the Case between WILLIAM STROTHER Gent. Plt. and GEORGE COLLEY Defendt., for twelve hundred & thirty nine pounds of tobacco due p Accot: WILLIAM MOORE the sd Defendts. Special Bail came into Court & delivered him up, afterwards the Defendt. appeared in Custody of EDWIN HICKMAN Gent. Sheriff and confessed Judgment for ye same with costs & an attorneys fee; It is therefore ordered that the sd Defendt. in Custody as aforesaid do pay unto ye sd Plantiff the same alias Exo.

- In the action of Trespass upon the Case between JOHN MERCER Plt. and ANDREW HARRISON Defendt., the same is continued to the next Court

- In the action of Debt between GEORGE TILLY, Mercht., Plt. and GOODRICH LIGHTFOOT, late Sheriff of Spotsylvania County, Gent. Defendt., for four pounds seven Shillings & six pence current money, and one hundred & forty four pounds of tobacco due by Judgment &c., the Defendt. appeared and suffered Judgment to pass against him for the same with costs & attorneys fee; It is therefore ordered that ye sd Defendt. do pay the said Plt. the same with costs & an attorneys fee alias Exo.

- In the action of Debt between THOMAS BYRN Plt. and GOODRICH LIGHTFOOT Gent. Defendt., for four thousand pounds of tobacco due by Bill, the same being agreed, Ordered that the suit be dismist

- In the action of Trespass upon the Case between JOHN HOLLADAY Plt. and GEORGE MUSICK Defendt., Judgmt. passed by Nil Dicit against ye sd Defendt.

- In the action of Debt between THOMAS GRAVES Plt. and RICHARD PARSLOW Defendt. for fourteen pounds current money damage, the Plt. failing to file his Declaration, ordered that ye same be dismist

- In the action of the Case between JOHN GORDEN Plt. and SAMUEL VAUGHN Defendt., for three pounds current money damage, the same order granted

- In the action of the Case between JOHN CHEW Plt. and NICHOLAS CHRISTOPHER Defendt., for two pounds two Shillings & eight pence current money due p Accot: the Defendt. appeared and confessed Judgment for the same with costs & attorneys fee; It is therefore ordered that the sd Defendt. do pay ye sd Plantiff the same with costs & an attorneys fee alias Execution

p.   Spotsylvania County Court 3d of September 1729
351   - In the action of Debt between OLIVER SEGAR Plt. and ANN JAMES, Admx. &c. of
       EDWARD SOUTHALL deceased, Defendt., on ye sd Defendts. motion oyer is granted
her

- In the action of Trespass upon the Case between JOSEPH COOPER Plt. and JOHN KILGORE Defendt., the same is continued

- In the action of Debt between JOHN ROBINSON Plt. and THOMAS ALLEN Defendt. the said Defendt. appeared and moved that time to the next Court to bring his Discount might be given him is granted, And Ordered that Judgment should pass for the Ballance due next Court

- In the action of Trespass upon the Case between HUGH FRENCH Plt. and WARREN BAWLDWIN Defendt., for fourteen pounds current money due by Accot: the Sheriff having made return that ye sd Defendt. is not to be found, Ordered that the suit be dismist

- In the Scire facias brought by CHARLES CHISWELL Plt. against FRANCIS LOVE and GOODRICH LIGHTFOOT Gent. late Sheriff, Defendts. for four pounds fifteen Shillings and a half penny current money & two hundred & fifty three pounds of tobacco due p Judgment &c., the Defendt. failing to appear to shew cause why Judgment should not be renewed to ye sd Plt. for ye same, Ordered that the sd Judgment be renewed for ye sd sum of four pounds fifteen shillings & a half penny current money and two hundred & fifty three pounds of tobacco with costs and an attorneys fee; It is therefore ordered that ye sd Defendts. do pay unto ye sd Plt. the same with costs and an attorneys fee alias Execution

- In the action of Trespass upon the Case between JOHN MERCER Plt. and RICHARD CHEEK Defendt., the Defendt. failing to appear and answer ye same, On motion of Plt. an order against ye sd Defendt. and his security is granted

- In the action of Trespass between RICE CURTIS JUNR. Plt. and JOHN SNELL JUNR. Defendt., on ye Defts. motion a Special Imparlance is granted

- In the action of the Case between JOHN GRAME Gent., Attorney of ALEXANDER SPOTSWOOD Esqr. Plt. and WILLIAM SMALLPEACE Defendt., on motion of ye sd Defendt. oyer is granted

- In the action of the Case between JOHN WIGLESWORTH Plt. and HENRY GOODLOE Gent. Defendt., the Plt. put in a demurrer and on the Defendts. motion time is given him to consider the same

- The Jury that were summonded and sworn in the suit between JOHN TALIAFERRO JUNR. Gent. and JOHN GRAME Gent. Defendt., failing to appear & deliver their Verdict, Ordered that the Sheriff do summonds them to appear at the next Court to deliver the same

- Ordered that the Court be adjourned till the Court in Course
                    WILLIAM HANSFORD

p.
352
- At a Court held for Spotsylvania County October y 7th Anno Domini 1729
                    Present

GOODRICH LIGHTFOOT   ROBERT SLATTER
JOHN TALIAFERRO   AMBROSE GRAYSON
WILLIAM HANSFORD   ABRAM FIELD   Gentn. Justices
WILLIAM BLEDSOE   ROBERT GREEN
JOSEPH BROCK

- On petition of GEORGE LANG in order to prove his rights to take up land according to his Majties. Royall Charter made Oath that he came into this Countrey about twelve years since in the Ship called the *MULBERRY* and that he brought REBECCA his Wife and that this is the first time of his proving their said Importations; Whereupon Certificates is ordered to be granted him of Rights to take up One hundred acres of land

- On petition of ANTHONY GOLDSON for more hands to be added to his gang on the Road that he is Overseer of, the same is rejected

- JOHN COOK acknowledged his Deeds of lease and release for land unto CHARLES STEVENS. likewise ANN the Wife of ye said JOHN (after being privately examined) acknowledged her right of Dower in the said land unto the said STEPHENS, at whose motion the same was admitted to record

- WALTER FRANCIS acknowledged his Deed of Gift for Goods andChatells unto
EDWARD PRICE, at whose motion the same was admitted to record

- JOHN LANDRUM acknowledged his Deed for Land to ROBERT THOMAS & MARY
LANDRUM, the Wife of ye sd JOHN, Power of Attorney being first proved p the Oathes of
WILLIAM BARTLETT and ROBERT BOURN to JOHN WALLER, afterwards ye sd WALLER
acknowledged ye sd MARYs right of Dower in the sd Land unto ye sd ROBERT THOMAS at
whose motion ye same was admitted to record

- JOHN TALIAFERRO Gent. acting Exr. of ROBERT TALIAFERRO deced, exhibitted
the account made up of ye sd Deceased Estate which was read & examined p the Court,
and ye said TALIAFERRO, Exr. as aforesaid, having made oath to the same, was approved
and ordered to be lodged in the Office

- On petition of JOHN GRAME Gent., in order to prove his right to take up Land
according to his Majties. Royall Charter made Oath that he came into this Countrey
about three years since and that he brought KATHERINE his Wife and two Sons named
GRANVILL & ALEXANDER, one Apprentice named JOHN MACKMATUR and one maid
Servant named ELIZABETH WEBSTER, and that this is the first ime of his proving their
said Importation; Whereupon Certificate is ordered to be granted him of Rights to take
up three hundred acres of land

- PHILLEMON CAVENAUGH, Overseer of the RAPPAHANOCK ROAD petitioning this
Court for Order and Directions where he may have Timber to build the Bridge ordered to
be build over the HAZLE RUN (p reason Mr. JAMES WILLIAMS Owner of ye land adjacent
have forewarned him to fall any trees of his) It is considered p the Court that their is
no great Occasion for building that Bridge, Ordered that the said petition be dismist

p.   Spotsylvania County Court 7th of October 1729
353   - On petition of PHILLEMON CAVENAUGH in behalf of his Son, CHARLES CAVE-
       NAUGH, to have his buildings works & Improvements &c. valued p two or more
men upon Oath (as the Law directs) with regard to the Accot: of Expences that he hath
been at in Seating a tract of four hundred acres of land in the Great Fork of RAPPA-
HANOCK RIVER, is granted, and Ordered that ROBERT GREEN, FRANCIS SLAUGHTER,
GEORGE HOME and BENJAMIN TAYLOR or any three of them (being first sworn before a
Majestrate of this County) do value the several kinds of buildings and Improvements
and on what part of the said land the same are and make return of their proceedings to
the next Court

- On motion of BENJAMIN PORTER, Overseer of the SOUTH WEST MOUNTAIN ROAD
for order and directions where he may have Timber to build the Bridge over the MINE
RUN (WM. EDDINS having forewarned him from falling any trees of his) It is ordered
that ye said BENJAMIN PORTER have liberty to agree with any person living the most
convenient to ye sd Bridge to buy Timber and build and repair the same on ye Cheapest
and best terms he can, and they to be paid for ye sd Timber by the County at the laying
of the next County Levy

- Present THOMAS CHEW, HENRY GOODLOE, Gentlemen Justices
- On ye petition of Mr. CHARLES CHISWELL & Partners about having Bridges over
the RIVERs PO & NY at the County Charge, the Gentlemen appointed having made
return & ye Agreement made about building the Bridge over the RIVER NY, but the
other part of the said order not being complyed with, Ordered that the same be continued to the next Court for the Gentlemen appointed to fully comply with the same &
make return thereof

- Ordered that the Sheriff do summonds a Grand Jury to tend the next Court to
swear and make their Presentments (if any) for the body of this County as the Law
directs

- The the Court proceeded to lay the County Levy. Vizt
Spotsylvania County is Dr.

Mens Names	Wolves Heads	By whom Granted	Tobacco
WILLIAM BELL	1	p AMBROSE GRAYSON Gent.	200
WILLIAM BLESDOE Ass: of EDWARD HALEY	4	p WILLIAM BLEDSOE Gent.	800
FRANCIS KIRKLEY Ass: of JACOB WALL	1	p ROBERT GREEN Gent.	200
ROBERT GREEN, Ass: of JOHN HEWS	1	p ROBERT GREEN Gent.	200
Ditto, Ass: of ELIZA. HEWS & JOHN HEWS	1	p Ditto	200
Ditto, Ass. of JONAS JENKINGS	1	p ABRAM. FIELD, Gent.	200
JOHN HOLLADAY, Ass. of ROBERT ANDREWS	1	p WILLIAM JOHNSON, Gent.	200
JOSEPH FOX	1	p ROBERT SLAUGHTER, Gent.	200
THOMAS GRAVES	1	p WILLIAM JOHNSON, Gent.	200
WILLIAM CRAWFORD Ass. of WILLM. STEPHENS	3	p JOHN TALIAFERRO, Gent.	600
ANN JAMES. Ass: of JOHN ROWSELL	1	p JOHN SCOTT, Gent.	200
WILLIAM SMITH, Ass: of ANDREW HARRISON	1	p WILLIAM SMITH, Gent.	200
NICHOLAS COPLAND	1	p WILLIAM HANSFORD, Gent.	200
WIATTE THOMAS	1	p ROBERT SLAUGHTER, Gent.	200
THOMAS DOWDEY	1	p Ditto	200
JOSEPH HAWKINGS	1	p JOHN SCOTT, Gent.	200
JOHN TRAVIS	1	p AMBROSE GRAYSON, Gent	200
	22		4400

p.   Spotsylvania County Court 7th of October 1729
354

Carried Over	Wolves Heads		Tobacco
To ZACHARY LEWIS, Ass. of WM. SMITH	1	p AMBROSE GRAYSON Gent.	200
Ditto, Ass. of RALPH HEWS	1	p ABRAM FIELD	200
JOHN DAVIS	1	p GOODRICH LIGHTFOOT	200
HENRY BERRY Ass. of GEORGE COLLEY	1	p WILLIAM BLEDSOE	200
Ditto Ass. of JOHN KITSON (?)	1	p WILLIAM JOHNSON	200
Ditto	1	p WILLIAM BLEDSOE	200
Ditto	4	p Ditto	800
JOHN TALIAFERRO, Ass. of WM. OFFILL	3	p JOHN SCOTT	600
Ditto. Ass. of JOHN ROWSELL	2	p Ditto	400
GOODRICH LIGHTFOOT, Ass. of RICHD. SHARP	1	p WILLIAM BLEDSOE	200
JAMES GARTON	1	p AMBROSE GRAYSON	200
	39	Ammounting to	7800

To Mr. Secretary CARTER	520
To Mr. ROBERT SPOTSWOOD for Keeping the FERRY at GERMANNA	2000
To Mr. JOHN GORDEN for keeping Prisoners, mending ye Prison, Candles, Small Beer, &c. as p his Account	2030
To JOHN WALLER as Clerk his yearly Sallary as p Law	1080
To Mr. WILLIAM SMITH for a Coroners fee of MICHAEL BERNARD	133
To Mr. EDWIN HICKMAN Sheriff his yearly Sallary as p Law	1080
To Ditto for summonding a Jury of Inquest & mending two Locks	110
To Majr. GOODRICH LIGHTFOOT for fetching ye County Surveyors Book &c.	500
To JOHN WIGLESWORTH for building BRIDGE over RIVER NY according to agreemt.	2000
To Cask & Conveniency of Ditto at 8 & 10 p cent	360

	Tobacco Plants	
To JOHN WALLER Ass. of WM. EDDINS for Timber to mend the MINE BRIDGE & Copy Order		158
To Mr. ZACHARY LEWIS for being Kings Deputy Attorney		1280
To the Admrs. of Capt. LARKIN CHEW deced for delinquents as p Accot:		438
To JOHN WALLER for Copys of the Laws &c. as p Accot:		2440
		14121
To Mr. JOHN KEY & DANIEL BROWN for counting	1,278,455	1065
To Mr. GEORGE HOME & BENJAMIN CAVE ditto	668,100	557
To Mr. WILLIAM BICKERS & JOHN CHRISTOPHER ditto	1,152,787	960
To Mr. GEORGE UTZ & MICHAEL COOK	136,525	114
To Mr. JOHN GRAYSON JUNR.. & JAMES WILLIAMS	978,822	816
TO Majr. GOODRICH LIGHTFOOT & Capt. ROBERT SLAUGHTER	560,669	468
To Mr. ROBERT GREEN & FRANCIS KIRKLEY	701,694	585
To Mr. JOHN FOSTER & ANTHONY FOSTER	1,016,367	848
	6,493,419	5413
		27337
To the Sallary to the Sheriff for Collecting 27337 lbs. Tobo at 10 p Cent		2734
		30071

Memorandum
1394/30071/ is 21 1/2 p Poll & 100 the fraction
1225/30071 after the Exempts 169 taken out is 24 1/2 p Poll & fraction due to the Sheriff 58 lbs.
The Country to pay for the Mine People exempted   3633 1/2

p   Spotsylvania County Court 7th of October 1729
355   - The Whole County Charge ammounting unto thirty thousand & seventy one
pounds of tobacco to be Levyed on Twelve hundred and Twenty five Tithables
(which are the True Quantity after the One hundred & sixty nine tithables belonging to
the IRON MINES Exempted by Law are taken out) comes to Twenty four & a half pounds
of tobacco p Poll (and fifty eight pounds of Tobacco, the fraction will be due to the
Sheriff. which EDWIN HICKMAN, Gent. Sheriff is ordered and Impowered to Collect and
receive the same from those to whom the said tithables or any of them do belong and
pay and satisfie the respective County Creditors, he having entered into bond with
GOODRICH LIGHTFOOT & JOSEPH BROCK Gent. his securitys as the Law directs, and in case
of non payment he is Impowered to levy the same by distress.
        - WILLIAM TODD Gent. and MARTHA his Wife, acknowledged their Deeds of Lease
and Release for land unto PHILLIP TODD Gent.. which at the motion of JOHN WALLER
JUNR. in behalf of ye sd PHILLIP, the same were admitted to record
        - On Information made to this Court p THOMAS CHEW Gent. that Capt. JOHN SCOTT
did in September last past swear Six Oaths in Saint Georges Parish in this County,
Ordered that ye sd SCOTT be fined Thirty shillings or three hundred pounds of tobacco
for the same with costs: It is therefore ordered that the said SCOTT do pay the said fine
or give Sufficient Caution for ye payment of the same at ye Laying the next Parish
Levy unto the Churchwardens of St. Georges Parish and pay costs
        - ROBERT TURNER. Deputy Sheriff. made return of the following Exo. Vizt.
THOMAS CARR's Exo. vs. WILLIAM RICHESON & CHEWs Admrs., for 16 lbs. Tobo: & L ..1..10
Currt. with 409 lbs. Tobo. costs
        - On petion of JOHN GORDEN, Overseer of the Road from the MARKED STONES to
GERMANNA for to have the WILDERNESS RUN BRIDGE built at ye County Charge (p reason
his gang Chiefly consisting of Coll. ALEXANDER SPOTSWOODs MINE PEOPLE which now
are Exempted p Law) is granted and Ordered that GOODRICH LIGHTFOOT. WILLIAM BLED-

SOE and ROBERT GREEN Gentlemen or any two of them, do agree with some person to build the same on the Cheapest Terms they can and make return of their proceedings to the next Court

- Ordered that all the Tithables which live in ye Fork be Discharged from serving under JOHN GORDEN, Overseer of the Road from the MARKED STONES to GERMANNA p reason the Bridge now being to be built on the County Charge

- Capt. WILLIAM HANSFORD & his Officer, JOHN GRAYSON JUNR., came into Court & took oaths & signed the Test as the Law directs, which was administred to them p GOODRICH LIGHTFOOT Gent.

- THOMAS CHEW & LARKIN CHEW, Admrs. &c. with the Will annexed of LARKIN CHEW deced, came into Court and suffered Judgment to pass to Collo. ALEXANDER SPOTS-WOOD for ten pounds two shillings & three pence current money due by Accot: with costs (when Assetts & Debts of greater Dignity are paid and satisfied) out of ye sd LARKIN CHEW Deced Estate in the hands of ye said Admrs. &c.

- Ordered that the Court be adjourned till the Court in Course

G: LIGHTFOOT

p.
356
<u>- At a Court held for Spotsylvania County November ye 4th 1729</u>
Present

GOODRICH LIGHTFOOT	JOHN SCOTT	
HENRY GOODLOE	ABRAHAM FIELD	Gentn. Justices
ROBERT SLAUGHTER		

- On petition of JOHN TRUSTOE to have his marke of Cattle & HOggs recorded which is a crop and four notches on the right ear and two holes in the left ear is granted

- On petition of EDWARD FRANKLYN to be discharged from being Overseer from Capt. JERIMIAH CLOWDERS ROAD to the CHURCH on the RIVER NY is granted and ordered that JOHN DURRETT do serve in his room

- On petition of ABRAHAM ABNEY, he is discharged from being Overseer of the Road from the COUNTY LINE to EAST NORTH EAST BRIDGE and ordered yt: GEORGE WOOD-ROFE do serve in his room

- On petition of THOMAS WEYLAND in order to prove his rights to take up land according to his Majties. Royall Charter made Oath that he came into this Countrey and brought his Wife. MARY. and two Children named JACOB and KATHERINE with him and that this is the first time of his proveing their said importations; Whereupon Certificate is ordered to be granted him of Rights to take up two hundred acres of land

- The Grand Jury according to summons appeared when called & being sworn for the body of this County and received their Charge, retired, & after some time returned & brought in the following Presentments, Vizt.

Mr. THOMAS JERMAN for makeing a breech of the Sabath p suffering his waggons & cattle to be drove on the Sabbath within two months last past

Wee also present FRANCIS ARNOLD for not frequenting his Parrish Church for the space of two months, within two months last past

Wee also present ROBERT ELLIS for swearing two oaths, within two months last past

Wee also present ANDREW DONOLSON for not frequenting his Parrish Church for the space of two months within the space of two months last past

FRANCIS SLAUGHTER, foreman

- Ordered that the severall people presented be summoned to the next Court to answer the said Presentments

- JAMES CANNON acknowledged his Deeds of Lease and Release for land unto JOSEPH COTTMAN, & MARY the Wife of the said CANNON (after being first examined) acknowledged her right of Dower of the said land to the said COTTMAN which were ordered to be recorded

- Present ROBERT GREEN Gentn.

- In the action of Trespass brought by JOHN TALIAFERRO JUNR. of CAROLINE COUNTY Gent., Plt. against JOHN GRAME Gentn. the Jury being called to appear & deliver in their verdict & severall of them failing to appear, Ordered that thay be fined according to Law if thay do not appear the next Court & shew good cause for their absence; afterwards p consent of each party the same is referred to the next Court for a new tryall p a new Jury

p.   Spotsylvania County Court 4th of November 1729
357   - In the action of Debt brought p THOMAS CARR JUNR. Plt. against THOMAS CHEW
      and LARKING CHEW. Admrs. with the Will annexed &c. of LARKIN CHEW deced,
Deefendts., for twelve pounds twelve shillings & three pence Sterlin, the Defendts. failing to appear, on motion of the Plt., Judgment is granted him against the Estate of the sd CHEW deced in the hands of the said Admrs. if thay fail to appear & answer the suit next Court

- In the action of Trespass on the Case brought p JAMES TAYLOR Gentn. against Ditto. Administrators, for Ten pounds ten pence seven shillings & two pence currant money and two thousand nine hundred and six pounds of tobacco, the same order is granted

- On petition of DAVID JONES in order to prove his rights to take up land according to his Majties. Royall Charter, made oath that he and his Wife, ELIZABETH, came into this Countrey and that it is the first ime of his proveing their said Importations, Whereupon Certificate is ordered to be granted them of Rights to take up One hundred acres of land

- Absent ABRAHAM FIELD, Gentn.

- In the action of Debt brought p JERIMIAH BRONAUGH JUNR. and ROSE his Wife, Admx. with the Will annexed &c. of JOHN DINWIDDIE deced, Plt. against ABRAHAM FIELD Defendt., who put in an Injunction in Chancery & desired that it might be received was granted. on which Mr. JOHN MERCER in behalf of the Plantifes desired time till the next Court to consider the same, which was granted him

- WILLIAM BARTLETT and WILLIAM BARTLETT. Assee. of SAMUEL BARTLETT, Plt. against HARRY BEVERLEY Defendt., on the action of Trespass upon the Case, the same is continued at the Defendts. costs

- On the Attachment obtained p WILLIAM RUSSELL against the Estate of EDWARD WINGFIELD, on the Plantifes motion the same is continued to the next Court

- In the action of Trespass upon the Case brought p THOMAS BENSON Plt. against JOSEPH SMITH Gentn. Defendt., Errors last Court being assighned for the stay of Judgment & referred to this Court for arguement and the Court haveing heard all on each side are of oppinion that ye Errors are not good, Therefore Judgment granted to ye Plantife against the Defendant for Twelve pounds currant money according to the Jurys Verdict with costs & an Atto. fee; On which the Defendant moved for leave to put in an Injunction in Chancery to stay Execution which was granted provided he lodged it in the Office ten days before the next Court, (JOHN WILKINGS entering himself security & assuming in Court to pay the Judgment if the Plt. were cast)

- On the motion of WILLIAM RUSSELL to have SILVANUS PUMPHARY Sale of a Negroe man named Cesar to him admitted to record is granted & ordered that the same be recorded

- On the Attachment obtained p JOHN DOWDEY against the Estate of RICHARD LEWIS for fiveteen hundred pounds of Tobacco, which the Plt. made out on oath to be due. Judgment is granted him for the same against the said LEWIS with costs & an attorneys fee; And the said Attachment being returned served in the hands of FRANCIS MICHAEL and JAMES HORSNAIL, the said MICHAEL appeared & on oath declared that he had in his possession of the said LEWIS Estate the severall things Vizt: one old Sadle & housing, one old duffell Coat, 1 pr. old leather Britches, 1 pr. old yarn hose; 1 old frying pan, 1 old bason, five spoons & a plate; one old bagg, five poultrey, one old box Iron, two blanketts, one old Rugg & one Bolster: Ordered that the Sheriff do sell the same p Outcry as the Law directs & deliver the same to the Plantife & JAMES HORSNAIL not appearing according to Summons, Ordered that he be attached to give an Accot: next Court what of the said LEWIS Estate he hath in his hands or possession at the time when the Attachment was served on him and make return of the proceedings to the next Court

- Ordered that the Court be ajoaurned till to Morrow morning at eight of the Clock   G. LIGHTFOOT

p.   Spotsylvania County Court 4th of November 1729
355   - JOHN TALIAFERRO and FRANCIS TALIAFERRO acknowedged their Deeds of Lease and Release for land unto BENJAMIN PORTER and at the motion of WILLIAM RUSSELL in the said PORTERs behalfe the same were admitted to record

- At a Court continued & held for Spotsylvania County November ye 5th 1729
Present

GOODRICH LIGHTFOOT	ROBERT SLAUGHTER	
HENRY GOODLOE	ABRAHAM FIELD	Gentn. Justices
JOHN SCOTT	ROBERT GREEN	

- GEORGE PROCTER acknowledged his Deeds of Lease and Release for land unto JOSEPH PARKER, at whose motion the same were admitted & ordered to be recorded

- On petition of WILLIAM RUSSELL in behalf of WILLIAM BEVERLEY Gentn. for leave of the Court to make an agreement with a man Servant of his named CHARLES FLOYD, to serve him two years and half after his time by Indenture is expired on the said BEVERLEY agreeing that the said FLOYD may marry his Servant, BARBARY CLINCH & she to be free at ye sd FLOYDs two years & half service after his indented time of service which will be on ye 22d of September 1732, and the said WILLIAM to maintain all their Children dureing their Servitude, the same is granted & agreed unto

- In the action of Trespass brought p JOSEPH SMITH Gentn. Plantife against THOMAS BENSON Defendt., for ten pounds Sterlin damage, issue being joyned and put to a Jury for Tryall p name JOHN GRAYSON JUNR., &c., who after being sworn &c. brought in their verdict Vizt. Wee of the Jury find for the Plantife twenty Shillings Sterlin damage, JOHN GRAYSON JUNR., foreman, which verdict at ye Plantifes motion was admitted to record & Judgment granted for the same with costs and an attorneys fee; Therefore ordered that the said Defendt. do pay unto the said Plantife the same alias Exo.

- On motion of Mr. ZACHARY LEWIS in behalfe of Mr. CHARLES CHISWELL Gentn. and divers other Adventurers in an IRON WORKE upon DUGLAS RUN in this County to have the order of the Generall Court bearing date October ye 24th 1729: recorded and that men may be appointed to veiw and value all such Timber as shall be necessary for

the building a Bridge over the RIVER PO according to ye sd Order, is granted, & ordered
that JOHN HOLLADAY, JOHN KEY & ROBERT KING or any two of them do appraise all such
Timber when the same shall be cutt down for ye building of the said BRIDGE and make
report of their proceedings to ye next Court
    - The Copy of ye Order of the Generall Court Vizt.

  At a General Court held for the Capitol, October the 24th 1729, CHARLES CHISWELL Gent.
in behalf of himself and divers other Adventurers in an IRON WORK upon DUGLASS
RUN in Spotsylvania County called FREDERICKSVILLE this day produced an order of the
Court of the said County dated the fifth of February last for laying out and making a
new Road from the said IRON WORK to a Landing on RAPPAHANOCK RIVER at the mouth
of the HASLE RUN between the lands of MAN PAGE Esqr. and Mrs. JAEL JOHNSON, according to the report of the Veiwers appointed by the said Court for that purpose persuant
to an Act of Assembly lately made and an order of the said Court made the first day of
April following for dividing the sd Road into precincts and appointing Surveyors for
the same and also another Order of the said Court dated the Sixth of August last for Repairing the Old Road and building Bridges over the

p.   Spotsylvania County Court 5th of November 1729
359 RIVERS NY and PO at the County Charge and an order for continuing the same
      made the Seventh of October following whereby as he suggested the former
orders were by the Inhabitants of the said County supposed to be sett aside and therfore
moved that the said New Road being in great measure already cleareld and a Bridge
being made over the RIVER NY might be cleared and compleated as being most convenient for the said IRON WORK and that a convenient Bridge might be built over the
RIVER PO at the Counties Charge, And the Court having heard the said CHISWELL and
also JOSEPH BROCK on behalf of the said Court, Thereupon do order that the order of the
said County Court made in August and October last be set aside and that the said orders
made in February and April last be confirmed and also that the Road therein mentioned
be continued and established as the Road from the said IRON WORK to the said Landing
on RAPPAHANOCK RIVER and be cleared and compleated as soon as the same can be con-
veniently done and that the said CHISWELL have leave at his own Expence to Build a
Substantial and Convenient Bridge over the RIVER PO and the said County Court at the
next Levy are to allow him his reasonable Charges and Disbursements about the same
and in the meantime to appoint fit persons to appraise the Timber which shall be
necessary for the building the said Bridge when the same shall be putt down to the end
the Owners thereof may be duly satisfied and forasmuch as it is of late disputed whether
surveyors of the Highways are by Law Impowered to take wood in the adjacent lands for
making and repairing such Bridges and Causeys as they are oblidged to make and
repair whereby the due execution of the Laws concerning Highways is likely more and
more to be obstructed, this Court have thought fit to declare their opinion that Surveyors of the Highways may lawfully take such wood for that purpose as is nearest and
next adjacent to the Bridges and Causeys which are to be made and repaired by them so
as they act therein with Caution and a Strict regard to the Interest of the owners of
such wood and do the least damage that can be to them
                              Cop: Test JNO. FRAUNCIS DCGC
    - Absent JOHN SCOTT Gentn. Justice
    - On the motion of JOHN SCOTT Gentn. Liberty is granted him to clear a BRIDLE
WAY from his Path that now is to the MOUNTAIN ROAD
        - Absent GOODRICH LIGHTFOOT, Gentn.
        - Present JOHN SCOTT Gentn.

- In the action of the Case brought p JERIMIAH MURDOCK Plt. against JONAS JENKINGS Defendt., for four hundred and forty five pounds of tobacco due p Accot: issue being joyned on the Defendts. plea & demurrer & referred to this Court for arguement, & the Court haveing heard all on each side are of oppinion that the said Plea is not good; Therefore Judgment is granted for the same with costs & an attorneys fee; It is therefore ordered that aye said Defendant do pay unto the said Plantife the same alias Exo.

- In the action of Debt brought p WILLIAM STROTHER Gentn. Plt. against THOMAS BYRN Defendt. for five hundred and thirty pounds of tobacco convenient, issue being joyned on the Defendts. plea & demurrer & referred for arguement & the Court haveing heard all on each side are of oppinion that the demurrer is not good, Therefore Judgment is granted ye Plt. for the sum with costs & an attorneys fee; It is therefore ordered that the Defendant do pay unto the Plantife the same alias Exo.

- Present WILLIAM BLEDSOE. Gentn. Justice

p.   Spotsylvania County Court 5th of November 1729
360   - On motion of JOHN WILKINGS, he is allowed for three days attendance as he was summoned an evedence for JOSEPH SMITH Gentn. vs. THOMAS BENSON & he haveing sworn to ye time; Its therefore ordered that the said SMITH do pay unto the said WILKINGS the same alias Exo.

- On motion of THOMAS GRAVES, the same order is granted him for Ditto agt. Ditto
- On motion of ANTHONY FOSTER, lthe same order is granted him for Ditto agt. Ditto

- In the action of Debt brought p RICHARD LONG, Assee; of JOHN SUTTON, Plt. against WILLIAM RUSSELL Defendt., for one thousand pounds of tobacco convenient in one Cask, the Defendant appeared & confessed Judgment for the same with costs & an attorneys fee; It is therefore ordered that the said Defendt. do pay unto the said Plantife the same alias Exo.

- In the action of the Case brought p RICHARD LONG Plt. against WILLIAM HUTCHESON, Defendt. the same is continued at the Plantifes costs

- In the action of Trespass upon the Case brought p THOMAS BENSON Plantife against JOSEPH SMITH Gentn. Defendt., for one hundred pounds Sterlin damage, issue being joyned & put to a Jury for tryall p name JOHN GRAYSON JUNR. &c., who after being sworn &c. brought in their verdict in these words, Wee of the Jury find for the Plantife one pound fiveteen shillings Sterlin damage, JOHN GRAYSON JUNR. foreman, which verdict at the Plantifes motion was admitted to record & Judgment granted for the same with costs and an attorneys fee; It is therefore ordered that the Defendt. do pay unto the said Plantife the said sum of one pound fiveteen shillings Sterlin with costs & an attorneys fee alias Exo.

- In the action of Trespass on the Case brought p JOSEPH SMITH Gentn. Plt. agt. WILLIAM RUSSELL Defendt., for fiveteen pounds Sterlin, issue being joyned & put to a Jury for tryall p name JOHN GRAYSON JUNR. &c., who after being sworn &c. brought in their verdict in these words, (Wee of the Jury find the said Plantife delivered the said Mare to the Defendant to goe the Journey within mentioned upon business he was employed about p the Plantife and others concerned in Company and that he never delivered the said Mare to the Plantife, Wee also find for the Plantife One pound Sterlin if the Law be for the Plantife, if not wee find for the Defendant, JOHN GRAYSON JUNR., foreman) which verdict is admitted to record and the matter of Law arising from the same is referred to the next for arguement

- In the action of Trespass on the CAse brought p WILLIAM STROTHER Gentn. Plt. against THOMAS BYRN Defendt. for two pounds & seven pence Currt. money due p Accot:

issue being joyned & put to the Court for trying the Defendts. demurrer, who haveing
heard all arguements on each side are of oppinion that the said demurrer is not good,
Therefore on motion of the Plantife, Judgment is granted him for the above sum with
costs and an attorneys fee; It is therefore ordered that the Defendant do pay unto the
Plantife the same alias Exo.

  - JOHN FOSTER, Deputy Sheriff, made return of ROBERT HYNDS Execution against
JOHN PIGG for one pound fourteen Shillings & 863 pds. of tobacco costs

  - On the Attachment obtained p WILLIAM RUSSELL agt. the Estate of JOHN
BLACKLEY for seven pounds ten Shillings currant money which he proved p his Oath
last Court & Judgment with costs & an attorneys fee for the same and the Sheriff
haveing made returne that WILLIAM BLEDSOE Gentn. Bill for six hundred pounds of
tobacco yt: was attached was p Outcry sold for two pounds two shillings currant money,
Ordered that the Sheriff do deliver the said money to the said RUSSELL & Judgmt.
granted for the ballance being five pounds Eight shillings with costs and an attorneys
fee; It is therefore ordered that the said BLACKLEY do pay the said RUSSELL the same
alias Exo. Exo. issued agt. BLACKLEYs body 9ber 7th 1730.

p. Spotsylvania County Court 5th of November 1729
361 - In the action of Trespass on the Case brought p JOSEPH ROBERTS Plt. against
  THOMAS ALLEN, the Plantife joyned the Defendts. plea & referred to the next
Court for tryall

  - In the action of Trespass on the Case brought p JOHN SNELL Plantife agt:
WILLIAM FRAZIER Defendt., issue joyned and referred for tryall

  - In the action of Trespass on the Case brought p MARY HAWKINGS & JOSEPH
HAWKINGS, Exrs. of JOHN HAWKINGS deced, Plts. against CHARLES GOODALL Defendt.,
issue joyned & referred to the next Court for tryall

  - In the Suit in Chancery brought p ROBERT SPOTSWOOD Plt. and THOMAS DAVIS
Defendt., the Complainant joyned the Defendants demurrer and the same is referred to
the next Court for arguement

  - On the petition of WILLIAM RUSSELL, Admr. with ye Will annexed &c. of WIL-
LIAM THOMPSON deced, for three cattle with calfes p their sides as GOODRICH LIGHTFOOT
Gentn. keeps & detains of the said THOMPSONs Estate, the Court haveing heard all evedence & arguements on each side are of oppinion that ye Cattle are now the Defendts. p
byeing them at an out cry sold p the Sheriff; therefore ordered that the said petition be
dismist

  - On motion of ROBERT GREEN Gentn., he is allowed for three days attendance as
he was summoned an evedence for WILLIAM RUSSELL, Admr. &c. of WILLIAM THOMP-
SON deced against GOODRICH LIGHTFOOT Gentn. (he haveing sworn to the time) It is
therefore ordered that the said RUSSELL, Admr. as aforesaid do pay the said GREEN the
same alias Exo.

  - On motion of JAMES CANNON (he haveing sworn to the time) is allowed the
same order as evedence for Ditto vs Ditto

  - The last Courts order which appointed GOODRICH LIGHTFOOT, WILLIAM BLED-
SOE and ROBERT GREEN Gentn. to agree with some workman to build a Bridge over ye
WILDERNESS RUN &c. at the County charge, not being complyed with, the same is con-
tinued to the next Court to compleat the same & make report

  - On motion of EDWIN HICKMAN Gent., he is allowed for three days attendance as
he was summoned an evedence for JOSEPH SMITH Gentn. against WILLIAM RUSSELL (he
haveing sworn to the time); It is therefore ordered that the said SMITH do pay unto the
said HICKMAN the same alias Exo.

- On motion of ROBERT GREEN Gentn. the same order is granted him for Ditto vs Ditto

- On motion of THOMAS HILL the same order is granted him for Ditto vs Ditto

- On motion of JOHN DUETT, he is allowed for three days attendance as he was summoned an Evedence for WILLIAM RUSSELL against JOSEPH SMITH Gentn., (he haveing sworn to the time); It is therefore ordered that the said RUSSELL do pay the said DUETT the same alias Exo.

- Ordered that the Court be adjourned to the Court in Course

G: LIGHTFOOT

p.
362

- At a Court held for Spotsylvania County December the second Anno Dom 1729

Present

HENRY WILLIS	ROBERT SLAUGHTER	
THOMAS CHEW	ABRAHAM FIELD	Gentlemen Justices
HENRY GOODLOE	ROBERT GREEN	
JOSEPH BROCK		

- On petition of JOHN GORDEN to have his ORDINARY LICENCE renewed, the same is granted, he giving bond & paying the Governours dues as the Law directs

- On petition of GEORGE MUSICK to be excused on going on ye Highways, the same is rejected

- On petition of DANIEL BROWN in behalf of himself & several others appointed to clear the Midle Precincts of the MINE ROAD from FREDERICKSVILLE to RAPPA-HANOCK RIVER &c., setting forth that they not being above twenty five tithables in the said precinct are not strength enough to clear the same and made Bridges and Causways as is required to be done, praying that more help may be assigned them to help clear the same &c. is rejected

- On petition of HENRY MARTIN to be discharged from being Overseer of the NASSANPONAX ROAD, the same is granted, and Ordered that CHARLES STEWARD do serve as Overseer in his room

- On petition of MRS. SUSANNA LIVINGSTON, Widow, to keep FERRY at FREDERICKSBURGH in this County, the same is rejected

- ISAAC BLEDSOE acknowledged his Deeds of Lease and Release for land unto BENJAMIN COTTMAN at whose motion the same was admitted to record

- On motion of HARRY BEVERLEY Gent. against WILLIAM MOORE, Overseer of the Road from COWLAND to the BRIDGE QUARTER that comes into GERMANNA ROAD for not keeping the said Bridge and grubing the said Road &c. as the Law directs, which being made appear to the Court, Ordered that he be fined fifteen Shillings for the same with costs, Therefore ordered that he pay ye sd HARRY BEVERLEY Gent. the Informer the same alias Execution

- On petition of JOHN THOMPSON about his Father, WILLIAM THOMPSON Deced Estate, in the hands of WILLIAM RUSSELL as Admr. &c. of the said Deced, the same being read, Ordered that ye sd petition be rejected

- Present GOODRICH LIGHTFOOT & WM. BLEDSOE, Gentn. Justices

- On petition of JOSEPH BLOODWORTH in order to prove his right to take up land acccording to his Majties. Royall Charter made oath that he and his Wife, MARY, came into this Countrey, And that this is the first time of his proving their said Importations, Whereupon Certificate is ordered to be granted them of Rights to take up One hundred acres of land

- On petition of WILLIAM RUSSELL to be discharged from being Overseer of the

Road from GERMANNA to the MOUNTAIN RUN BRIDGE in the Fork of the RAPPAHANOCK RIVER, the same is granted, and ordered that SAMUELL BALL do serve as Overseer in the room of ye sd RUSSELL

    - On motion of Coll. HENRY WILLIS to have a Road from his MILL in ye Fork of RAPPAHANOCK RIVER to GERMANNA, the same is granted, And Ordered that ROBERT GREEN, WILLIAM RUSSELL and FRANCIS KIRKLEY Gent. do veiw, lay out and mark the nearest & best way and make return of their proceedings to the next Court

p.   <u>Spotsylvania County Court 2d of December 1729</u>
363   - In the action of Debt between the Honble. ALEXANDER SPOTSWOOD Esqr. Plt. and ANDREW HARRISON Defendt., for five pounds & eleven pence and six hundred and ninty pounds of Tobacco due by Judgment &c., issue being joyned and put to a Jury for tryall p name JOHN GRAYSON &c., who after being sworn & heard all evedences &c. retired and brought in their Verdict in these words; We of the Jury find for the Defendt. RICHARD LONG, foreman, which verdict at the Defendts. motion was admitted to record and ordered that the suit be dismsit with costs and an attorneys fee; It is therefore ordered that ye sd Plt. pay the said Defendt. his costs and an attorneys fee alias Execution

    - On the Attachment obtained p MARY HAWKINS, Widow, against the Estate of THOMAS TYLER. THOMAS YATES not appearing p reason he was disabled p the bites of a Dog, ordered that ye same be continued to the next Court for ye sd YATES to appear

    - In the action of Debt between GEORGE PROCTER Plt. and JOHN YOUNG Defendt., the Attachment being returned not served by the Sheriff, on the Plts. motion the same is continued to be served in the hands of RICHARD CHEEK to the next Curt

    - In the action of Debt between JONATHAN HOOD Plt. and ALEXANDER SPOTWOOD Esqr. Defendt., ye sd Defendt. craved time to mend his plea which is granted, he paying costs & puting ye sd in a week before next Court

    - ROBERT TURNER, Deputy Sheriff, made return of the following Executions, Vizt. GEORGE TILLY, Mercht., agst. GOODRICH LIGHTFOOT Gent. &c. for £. 4...7...6 and 144 pds. of Tobo with 288 pds Tobo. costs; RICHARD LONG, Assee. of JNO. SUTTON agst. WILLIAM RUSSELL for 1000 pds of Tobacco and 283 costs

    - JOHN CHAMBERS, Deputy Sheriff of STAFFORD COUNTY, returned the following Execution. WILLIAM RUSSELL agst. JOHN BLACKLEY for £ 5...8 Currt. money and 404 pds Tobo: costs.

    - In the action of Trespass upon the Case between JOHN WALLER Plt. and EDWARD WINGFIELD Defendt., for twelve hundred seven and half pounds of Tobo: due p Accot:, An order being confirmed against the said Defendt. in Custody of EDWIN HICKMAN, Gent. Sheriff, for what should appear due by Writ of Enquiry last Court, and a Jury being Impannelled and sworn this p name RICHARD LONG &c. who haveing heard all arguements &c. brought in their verdict in these words: We of the Jury have found for the Plantife twelve hundred seven and a half pounds of tobacco damage, RICHARD LONG, foreman; which verdict at the Plts. motion was admitted to record and Judgment granted for the same with costs and an attorneys fee; It is therefore ordered that the said Defendt. in Custody as aforesaid pay the said Plt. the same alias Execution

    - In the action of the Case between JOHN TALIAFERRO Gent. Plt. and WILLIAM BECKHAM, Defendt., the same is continued at the Defendants costs

    - On motion of JAMES CANNEY, he is allowed for five days attendance as he was summoned an evedence for ALEXANDER SPOTSWOOD Esqr. against ANDREW HARRISON and for four times comeing and going thirty miles and Eight ferriages at seven pence half penny each ferriage (he having sworn to the same); It is therefore ordered that ye said SPOTSWOOD do pay ye sd CANNEY the same with costs alias Exo.

- In the action of the Case between BENJAMIN GRAYSON by his next Friend, JOHN
GRAYSON, Plt. against HARRY BEVERLEY Gent. Defendt., the same is postponed till tomorrow morning

p.   Spotsylvania County Court 2d of December 1729
364   - In the action of Debt between WILLIAM STROTHER Gent. Plt. and JOHN HEWS
       Defendt., the plurias capias being returned p the Sheriff not executed, which on
ye Plts. motion the same is ordered to be continued to the next Court
       - In the action of Debt between GEORGE TILLY Plt. and WILLIAM PERRY Defendt.,
for one pound eleven Shillings and six pence current money due by Bill, the same
being agreed, ordered that the said suit be dismist
       - On motion of Mr. BENJAMIN WINSLOW, he is allowed for four days attendance
as he was summoned an evedence for ALEXANDER SPOTSWOOD Esqr. against ANDREW
HARRISON and three times comeing and going seventy miles; It is therefore ordered
that ye said SPOTSWOOD do pay the said WINSLOW the same with costs alias Execution
       - Mr. EDMUND BAGG the same order granted for three days & twice comeing and
going seventy miles
       - Ordered that the Court be adjourned till to Morrow morning at nine of the
Clock   HENRY WILLIS

       - At a Court continued and held for Spotsylvania County December the third
Anno Dom. 1729   Present
       THOMAS CHEW   JOSEPH BROCK
       HENRY GOODLOE   JOHN SCOTT   Gentlemen Justices

       - In the action of the Case between BENJAMIN GRAYSON by his next Friend, JOHN
GRAYSON, Plt. against HARRY BEVERLEY Gent. Defendt. for two pounds Eight shillings &
one penny half penny current money due by Accot, issue being joyned, on the
Defendts. Demurrer and put to the Curt for tryall, who having heard and considered all
arguements are of oppinion that the said Demurrer is good; Therefore ordered that the
suit be dismist with costs and an attorneys fee; It is therefore ordered that ye sd Defendt.
do recover against ye sd Plt. his costs with an attorneys fee alias Execution
              - Present GOODRICH LIGHTFOOT, ROBERT SLAUGHTER, Gentlemen Justices
       - In the action of Trespass upon the Case between JAMES McCOLLOUGH Plt. and
EDWIN HICKMAN Gent., Sheriff, Defendt., the Plt. joyned ye sd Defendts. plea and
demurrer and referred to the next Court for tryall
       - In the action of Detinue between GEORGE NIX Plt. and EDWARD PRICE Defendt.,
who after having liberty to plead divers matters, put in a plea and the Suit is continued
p reason of ye Plts. attorney being sick to ye next Court
       - On the Attachment obtained by WILLIAM RUSSELL, Admr. of the Estate of WIL-
LIAM THOMPSON deced, with the Will annexed, against DENNIS MORGAIN for seven
hundred and sixty pounds of Tobo. due by Accot: the said Admr. &c. having swore that
he found ye sd Accot: so stated in ye sd deceased papers, Judgment is granted for the
same with costs and an attorneys fee; And JOHN CARDER appearing according to summonds and on Oath declared that he had two hundred and eighty pounds of tobacco &
eight shillings & ten pence current money of ye sd MORGAINs Estate, Ordered that the
said CARDER do deliver the same to the sd Admr. &c. And it is further ordered that ye sd
Attachment be continued and that WILLIAM RICHESON and JAMES MORGAIN be attached
to the next Court

p.   Spotslylvania County Court 3d of December 1729

365   - In the action of Debt between GEORGE HOME Plt. and WILLIAM RUSSELL Defendt
        for one thousand pounds of tobacco due by Bill, the Defendts. Errors assigned for
stay of Judgment on the Jurys verdict last Court being argued this, And the Court
having heard all the arguements on each side are of oppinion that the said Errors are
not good; Therefore ordered that Judgment be granted for the same according to the
Jurys verdict which is one thousand pounds of tobacco with costs and an attorneys fee;
It is therefore ordered that the said Defendt. do pay the said Plt. the same alias Execution
        - In the action of Trespass upon the Case between JAMES JONES Plt. and EDWARD
WINGFIELD Defendt., the same is continued
        - In the action of Trespass upon the Case between WILLIAM WOODFORD Gent. Plt.
and JOHN TALIAFERRO Gent., Exr. of ROBERT TALIAFERRO deced, Defendt., continued
        - In the action of Debt between ALEXANDER MACKFARLAND Plt. and THOMAS
CHEW and LARKIN CHEW, Admrs. with the Will annexed of LARKIN CHEW Gent. late
Sheriff, deced, Defendt., the same is continued at ye Plts. costs
        - In the action upon the Case between GEORGE HOME Plt. and CHARLES DUETT
JUNR. Defendt., the said Defendt. put in a plea and time given the Plt. to consider the
same
        - In the action of Debt between CHARLES BURGES Plt. and OWEN HUMPHREYS
Defendt., the Sheriff having returned the plurias capias not executed, on the Plts.
motion the same is continued
                - Present ABRAHAM FIELD, Gent. Justice
        - In the action of Debt between JOHN SMITH Plt. and GEORGE HOME and WM.
MOORE Defendts., the said Plt. put in a replication which ye sd Defendts. joyned and the
tryall thereof is referred to the next Court
        - In the action of Debt between JOHN SMITH Plt. and WILLIAM MOORE Defendt.,
the same order
        - In the action of Debt between LYONEL LYDE of the City of BRISTOL, Mercht., Plt.
and JOHN TALIAFERRO Gent., Exr. of ROBERT TALIAFERRO deced, Defendt., the same is
continued at ye Plts. costs
        - In the action of Trespass upon the Case between WILLIAM RUSSELL, Admr. &c.
with the Will annexed of WILLIAM THOMPSON deced, Plt. and ANDREW GLASPE Defendt.,
for seven hundred & seventy five pounds of tobacco damage, the Veiwers appoint by
the last Courts order having made return that there was work done by the said deced for
ye sd Defendt. to the value of two hundred and fifty pounds of tobacco; Therfore Judgment passed for the same with costs and an attorneys fee; It is therefore ordered that
ye said Defendt. pay the said Plt. the said sum of Two hundred & fifty pounds of tobacco
with costs and an attorneys fee alias Execution
        - In the action of Trespass upon ye Case between JOHN HOLLADAY Plt. and
GEORGE MUSICK Defendt., (Mr. ZACHARY LEWIS ye sd Plts. Attorney affirmed to this
Court that ye said Suit was agreed), but afterwoard the Defendt. put in a plea which ye
Plt. joyned and referred to the next Court for tryall
        - In the action of Debt between OLIVER SEGAR Plt. and ANN JAMES, Admx. &c. of
EDWARD SOUTHALL deced, Defendt., put in a plea and time given the Plt. to consider the
same
        - In the action of Trespass upon the Case between JOSEPH COOPER Plt. and JOHN
KILGORE Defendt. for five pounds current money damage, the suit being agreed,
ordered that the same be dismist

p.
366

Spotsylvania County Court 3d of December 1729

- In the action of the Case between JOHN GRAME, Attorney of ye Honble. ALEXANDER SPOTSWOOD, Plt. and WILLIAM SMALLPEACE Defendt., the Defendt. put in a plea after having liberty to plead divers matters, and on ye Plts. motion time is granted him to consider the same

- In the action of Debt between JOHN ROBINSON Plt. and THOMAS ALLING Defendt. for three pounds one Shilling & four pence Cash and one hundred and forty two pounds of tobacco due by Bill, Judgment passed against the said Defendt. for the same with costs and an attorneys fee; It is therefore ordered that ye said THOMAS ALLING do pay the said JOHN ROBINSON the same with costs and an attorneys fee alias Exo.

- In the action of Trespass upon the Case between JOHN MERCER Plt. and RICHARD CHEEK Defendt. for three hundred and ninty three pounds of tobacco due p Accot: And the said Plt. having made Oath that three hundred and forty eight pounds of tobacco was the ballance due to him, And an order having last Court passed against the said Defendt. and JOHN FOSTER, his security, for ye sd Defendts. non appearance and he now failing to appear when called this, the said order is confirmed for the same with costs and an attorneys fee; It is therefore ordered that the said Defendant and his security pay the said MERCER the same alias Exo.

- In the action of trespass between RICE CURTIS JUNR. and JOHN SNELL JUNR. Defendt., the said Defendt. put in a plea which the Plt. joyned and the tryall thereof is referred to the next Court

- In the action of the Case between JOHN WIGLESWORTH Plt. and HENRY GOODLOE Defendt., the said Defendt. joyned the Plts. demurrer and referred to the next Court for arguement

- In the action of trespass upon the Case between WILLIAM HACKNEY Plt. and JOHN CARDER Defendt. for two hundred and ninty seven pounds of tobacco due by Accot: the suit being agreed, ordered that the same be dismist

- In the action of Debt between DENNIS LINDSEY Plt. against JOHN DUETT Defendt. the sid Defendt. failing to appear when called to answer the same, on the Plts. motion an order is granted against ye sd Defendt. and his security

- In the action of the Case between WALTER ANDERSON Plt. and ROBERT EVANS Defendt. the Defendt. failing to appear when called to answer the same, On ye Plts. motion an order is granted agst. ye sd Defendt. in Custody of EDWIN HICKMAN, Gent. Sheriff

- In the action of Debt between JOHN GEORGE KAUFMAN Plt. and GEORGE POPPERWELL Defendt., for six pounds current money due by Bill, the Plt. craved special bail of ye sd Defendt. which was granted, and JOHN TALIAFERRO JUNR. Gent. entering himself special bail for the said Defendt., confessed Judgment for the same with costs and an attorneys fee; It is therefore ordered that ye sd Defendt. do pay the said Plt. the same with costs and an attorneys fee alias Exo.

- On motion of JOHN MERCER, Attorney & in behalf of EDWARD PRICE, for leave of the Court to put in an Injunction in Chancery to stop the issuing of an Execution as GEORGE HOME obtained against the said PRICE in this Court, was granted and renewed (HARRY BEVERLEY Gent. enering himself security in behalf of the sd PRICE to pay all Costs &c. if should be cast) afterwards the said HOME craved time to consider the said Injunction which was granted

- In the action of Covenant between WILLIAM SMALLPEACE Plt. and JOHN GRAME Defendt., the said Defendt. craved leave to plea divers matters which is granted, And on the Plts. motion time given to consider the said plea

- In the action of Trespass upon the Case between ANDREW GLASPE Plt. and

RICHARD CHEEK Defendt., the Sheriff having returned a Copy Left, on the Plts. motion an alias capias is granted

p.   Spotsylvania County Court 3d of December 1729
367   - In the action of Trespass upon the Case between WILLIAM HACKNEY Plt. and JOHN DUETT Defendt., for eleven hundred & fifty nine pounds of tobacco due p Accot:, the Suit being agreed, ordered that the said be dismist

    - In the action of Debt between Our Sovereign Lord the King Plt. and EDWARD PIGG and CHARLES FALKS PIGG Defendt., the said Defendt. put in a demurrer, and on the said Plts. motion time is granted him to consider the said demurrer

    - In the action of Trespass upon the Case between DAVID MITCHELL Plt. and WILLIAM MOORE Defendt., on ye sd Defendts. motion a special Imparlance is granted

    - In the action of Debt between THOMAS CARR JUNR., Plt. and DENNIT ABNEY JUNR. Defendt. for twenty pounds Sterling money due by Bill, the said Suit being agreed, ordered that the same be dismist

    - In the action of Debt between GEORGE HOME Plt. and WILLIAM RUSSELL Defendt the Sheriff having returned a Copy Left; On ye Plts. motion an alias capias is granted

    - In the action of Debt between WILLIAM RUSSELL, Admr. &c. with the Will annexed of WILLIAM THOMPSON deced. Plt. and JOHN PENDERGRASS Defendt., the said Defendt. failing to appear and answer when called, On the Plts. motion an order is granted against ye sd Defendt. and his security

    - In the action of Debt between GOODRICH LIGHTFOOT Gent. &c. Plt. and RICHARD CHEEK Defendt., the Sheriff having returned a Copy Left, On ye sd Plts. motion an alias capias is granted

    - In the action of Debt between ROBERT EVANS, Assignee of RICHARD BLANTON, Plt. and DENNIS LORDEN, Defendt. for one thousand pounds of tobacco damage, there being no declaration filed, Ordered that the same be dismist

    - In the Ejectione Firme between JOHN DOE Plt. and RICHARD ROE Defendt., THOMAS SMITH, Lessor, It is ordered that unless the Defendt. or those under him he claims do appear at ye next Court to be held for this County and plead the generall issue and enter into rule to confess Lease entry & Ouster and insist only upon the Title at tryall, Judgment shall be entered for ye said Plantiff and his Majties. Writ of Habere facias Possessionem awarded

    - In the action of Trespass upon the Case between JOHN MERCER Plt. and ANDREW HARRISON Defendt., for twenty pounds current money damage, the said suit being agreed, Ordered that the same be dismist

    - On motion of JOHN GRAME Gent., Attorney & in behalf of Collo. ALEXANDER SPOTSWOOD, for the Clerk of the Court to deliver unto him out of his office all the originall papers, Letters and the Judgments as the said GRAME, Attorney aforesaid, Lodged in the Clerkes Office as he brought Suit for against ANDREW HARRISON and was dismissed this Court, Likewise the Receipt for two hogsheads of tobacco that JAMES KENNY produced in Court as was pretended to be Shipt. of p the Revd. Mr. JOHN BAGGs Order as the said HARRISON pasd. the said BAGG; Its Ordered that the Clerk do deliver the same unto ye said JOHN GRAME Gent., Attorney as aforesaid, after having first recorded the same

    - In the action of Trespass and assault between JOHN FOSTER, Deputy Sheriff of Spotsylvania County, Plt. and JOSEPH PARKER Defendt., put in a plea after having Liberty to plea divers matters, and on ye Plts. motion time is granted him to consider the same

- In the action of the Case between JOHN CHAMPE Plt. and ROBERT EVANS Defendt., the said Defendt. failing to appear when called and answer the same, On the Plts. motion an order against the sd Defendt. in Custody of EDWIN HICKMAN Gent. Sheriff is granted

p.   Spotsylvania County Court 3d of December 1729
368   - In the action of the Case between ALEXANDER McFARLAND Plt. and JOHN WATT-
          FORD Defendt., the Sheriff having returned not executed, On the Plts. motion an alias capias is granted him

- On the petition of MOSLEY BATTALEY Plt. agst. THOMAS JARMAN Defendt., for three pounds eleven shillings current money, the same being agreed, ordered that ye sd Petition be dismist

- On the petition brought by HENRY CONNYERS Plt. against JOHN DAWLEY & JOHN KIMBROW Defendts., for two hundred pounds of tobacco & Cask convenient due by Bill, Judgment passed against the said KIMBROW for the same with costs and an attorneys fee It is therefore ordered that ye sd KIMBROW do pay the said CONNYERS the sum of two hundred pounds of tobacco & cask convenient with costs and an attorneys fee alias Execution

- In the action of Debt between THOMAS CARR JUNR. and ABRAHAM ABNEY Defendt. for seven pounds current money due by Bill, the suit being agreed, Ordered that the same be dismist

- In the action of Trespass between WILLIAM HOLLOWAY Plt. and EDWARD PRICE Defendt. on ye sd Defendts. motion a Special Imparlance is granted

- In the action of Trespass between JOHN BOND Plt. and JOHN MULKEY Defendt. for one thousand pounds of tobacco damage, the suit being agreed, Ordered that the same be dismist

- In the action of Trespass upon the Case between GEORGE TILLY Plt. and JAMES HOLLOWAY Defendt., the said Defendt. failing to appear and answer when called, On ye Plts. motion an order against ye sd Defendt. and his security is granted him

- In the action of Debt between JAMES McCULLER Plt. and GEORGE POPPERWELL Defendt., for one thousand pounds of tobacco damage, no declaration being filed, Ordered that the same be dismist

- In the action of Trespass upon the Case between GEORGE WOOD Plt. and RICHARD PARSLOW Defendt., for Eight hundred pounds of Tobacco damage, the same order granted

- On the Attachment obtained by THOMAS PHILLIPS Plt. against the Estate of RICHARD CORNELIUS for one pound fifteen Shillings current money, the said Plantiff faiing to prosecute the same, Ordered that the said Attachment be dismist

- On the Attachment obtained p JAMES GARTON against the Estate of RICHARD CORNELIUS the same is continued

- THOMAS JARMAN being called to answer ye Presentment of the Grand Jury for making a breach of the Sabbath p suffering his Waggons & Cattle to be drove on the Sabbath, the Sheriff delivered a Letter from him directed to the Court wherein he excused himself & set for the necessity that Occasioned that Accident, On which the Court referred the matter to the next Court for him to make Affidavitt of the same

- FRANCIS ARNOLD not appearing when called according to Summonds to answer the Presentment of the Grand Jury for not frequenting his Parish Church for the space of two months September and October last past, Ordered that the said FRANCIS ARNOLD be fined Ten Shillings or One hundred pounds of Tobacco for the same with costs; It is therefore ordered tha the said ARNOLD do pay the said fine or give sufficient caution for the payment of the same at ye laying the next Parish Levy unto the Churchwardens of St. Georges Parish, Otherwise if not able to pay the same to have twenty lashes on his bare back and pay costs

- ROBERT ELLIS ditto for swaring two Oathes within the space of two months last past, the same order granted

- ANDREW DONELSON ditto for absenting himself from his Parish Church for the space of two months last past, the same order granted

p.   Spotsylvania County Court 3d of December 1729
369   - On the Attachment obtained by WILLIAM RUSSELL against the Estate of ED-
        WARD WINGFIELD for four hundred and ninty six pounds of Tobo: and three Shillings current money, the said Plt. failing to prosecute the said Attachment, Ordered that the same be dismist

- In the action of Trespass upon the Case between THOMAS BENSON Plt. and JOSEPH SMITH Gent. Defendant, the same is continued at the Defendts. costs

- On the Attachment obtained by JOHN DOWDEY against the Estate of RICHARD LEWIS for fifteen hundred and fifty pounds of tobacco, and ye Plt. having made out the same to be due on Oath, Judgment for the same with costs and an attorneys fee was last Court granted him, And the Sheriff having returned that the things attached was sold for two hundred forty five and a half pounds of tobacco and JAMES HORSNAIL appearing according to summonds and on Oath declared that he had in his hand of ye sd LEWIS's Estate one pound one shilling & six pence which being by ye Court stated in tobacco at Ten shillings p hundred comes to two hundred and fifteen pounds of tobacco, Ordered that the Sheriff and the said JAMES HORSNAIL do deliver the Plt. the same And that Judgment be granted him for the Ballance which is one thousand and eighty nine & a half pounds of tobacco with costs and an attorneys fee against the said Defendt.; It is therefore ordered that ye sd LEWIS do pay the said DOWDEY the same with costs & an attorneys fee alias Exo.

- In the action of Trespass upon the Case between JOSEPH SMITH Gent. Plt. and WILLIAM RUSSELL Defendt., for fifteen pounds Sterling damage, the same being last Court put to a Jury which having brought in a special verdict was referred to this for arguing the matters of Law arising thereon, And the Court having heard all argue-ments on each side, and considered the same, are of oppinion that the Law is for the Plantiff; Therefore Judgment is granted for One pound Sterling (which was the Jurys verdict) with costs & an attorneys fee alias Execution

- On the Injunction in Chancery brought by ROBERT SPOTSWOOD againt THOMAS DAVIS to stop the Issuing of an Execution on a Judgment obtained in this Court on the fourth day of September in the year of our Lord One thousand seven hundred & twenty eight, by ye said THOMAS DAVIS against the said SPOTSWOOD, to which the Respondent, DAVIS, put in a demurrer which was joyned by ye Complt. and being argued by the Court are of Oppinion that the said Demurrer is not good; And therefore decreed that the said Injunction be continued until the said DAVIS do answer the same, from which Judgment the said DAVIS appealled, which was granted him, he having entered into recognizance with JOHN BOND his security, to answer and prosecute the same before the Honble the Generall Court next on the Eighth day thereof

- THOMAS DAVIS and JOHN BOND did in Court enter in recognizance & assumed on the penalty of Ten pounds current money each payable unto ROBERT SPOTSWOOD to appear and prosecute his, the said DAVIS, appeal against the said ROBERT SPOTSWOOD before the Honble the Generall Court next on the eighth day thereof

- A copy of the Receipt delivered into Court p JAMES CENNY at the tryall of the suit then depending between Coll. ALEXANDER SPOTSWOOD & ANDREW HARRISON Vizt.
delivered to me the Subscriber by JAMS. CENNY two haskide of tobaco wich be Longs to Mr. REVD. JOHN BAG wich was received of Mr. ANDRE HARRESON by me   CHARLES HOBSON
May the 6: 1726
- Ordered that the Court be adjourned to the Court in Course
THOS: CHEW

p.   - At a Court held for Spotsylvania County on Tuesday February ye 3: 1729
370   Present
GOODRICH LIGHTFOOT   JOHN SCOTT
HENRY GOODLOE   ABRAM FEILD   Gentn. Justices
ROBERT SLAUGHTER   ROBERT GREEN

- JOSEPH BROCK Gentn. warrant as he granted on ye Complaint of PATRICK BOLDING against SARAH, the Wife of WILLIAM BRADBOURN, and their Recognizance &c. being returned to this Court for further tryall & examination about her Misbehaviour, the Court having heard the Evedences and both parties, are of oppinion that the said SARAH BRADBOURN be committed into the Sheriff Custody and there to remain till she enter into Bond of Fifty pounds current money & security for her good behaviour a year and a day and pay costs; Likewise the said SARAH BRADBOURN Swearing the peace against ye said BOLDING, Ordered that he be in the Sheriffs custody and there to remain till he give bond and security of fifty pounds current money for keeping the peace a yar and a day and pay costs
- On motion of JOSEPH WHITE, he is allowed for one days attendance as he was summoned an evedence for SARAH, the Wife of WILLIAM BRADBOURN, against PATRICK BOLDING; It is therefore ordered that the said BRADBOURN pay the said WHITE the same alias Execution
- JOHN ASHER acknowledged his Deeds of Lease and Release for land unto GEORGE HOME at whose motion the same is admitted to record
- GEORGE HOME acknowledged his Deeds of Lease and Release for land unto JAMES ASHER, at whose motion the same was admitted to record
- Present THOMAS CHEW, Gent., Justice
- RICHARD CHEEKs Deed for land unto JOHN MILLER of ESSEX COUNTY was proved p the oaths of WILLIAM BARTLETT, JOHN PARKES and JOHN MILLER JUNR., Likewise JANE CHEEKs Power of Attorney being first proved to WILLIAM BARTLETT p the Oaths of JOHN MILLER JUNR. and JOHN PARKES, the said BARTLETT afterwards acknowledged her right of Dower of the said land unto ye sd MILLER, at whose motion the same were admitted to record
- RICHARD CHEEKs Deeds of Lease and Release for Land unto JOHN MILLER of CAROLINE COUNTY was proved p the Oaths of JOHN MILLER, JOHN PARKES and JOSEPH RETTERFORD, Likewise JANE CHEEKs Power of Attorney to WILLIAM BARTLETT being first proved by the oaths of JOHN MILLER and JOHN PARKES, afterwards the said BART-LETT acknowledged her right of Dower to ye sd MILLER at whose motion the same is admitted to record
- On petition of WILLIAM MOORE, he is discharged from being Overseer of the Road from COWLAND to ye BRIDGE QUARTER that comes into GERMANNA ROAD, And Ordered that JOSEPH WILLIAMS do serve as Overseer in his room; And that all the Tithables which served under ye sd MOOR doe help the said WILLIAMS to clear the same

- On petition of JAEL JOHNSON to Keep ORDINARY at her Dwelling House in this County is granted, She giving bond and paying the Governours dues as the Law directs &c.

- On petition of CHARLES STEVENS and severall others to have the Road that Liberty was given them to clear from Mr. AUGUSTINE MOORE's Quarter in the Fork of PAMUNKEY to Capt. JERIMIAH CLOWDERs ROLING ROAD drop, that not suiting the Inhabitants, and that Capt. JERIMIAH CLOWDERs ROLING ROAD way be continued up the Ridge in the sd Fork of PAMUNKEY, the most costs and Covenient way towards ye MOUNTAINS as farr as the people in those parts are inhabitted, is granted and ordered that JOHN COOK, CHARLES STEVENS, DAVID CAVE, JOHN HENDERSON and THOMAS COOK have liberty to clear the same.

- Absent THOMAS CHEW Gent., Justices

p. Spotsylvania County Court 3d of February 1729
371 - On petition of JOHN BOND against THOMAS CHEW and LARKIN CHEW, Admrs. &c. of LARKIN CHEW Gent., late Sheriff, deced, for a claim of two hundred & eighty seven pounds of tobacco which was allowed p ye County as he was Tob: Counter. THOMAS CHEW appearing and pleaded that ye sd claim was paid to ye sd Petitioner. Ordered that ye sd petition be continued to the next Court for the said Admr. &c. to make appear how ye same was paid

- In the action of Trespass upon the Case between WILLIAM WOODFORD Gent. Sheriff of CAROLINE COUNTY, Plt. and GEORGE WOODROFFE Defendt., for three thousand pounds of tobacco damage, the said Defendt. came into Court and confessed Judgment for twelve hundred and fourteen pounds of tobacco to be paid in cask convenient with costs and an attorneys fee, It is therefore ordered that the said Defendt. do pay unto the said Plantiff the same with costs and an attorneys fee alias Execution

- Then the Court adjourned till to Morrow moring at eight of the Clock

- At a Court held for the Proof of Publick Claims in Spotsylvania County on Tuesday February the third 1729   Present
GOODRICH LIGHTFOOT   ROBT. SLAUGHTER
HENRY GOODLOE   JOHN SCOTT   Gentlemen Justices
                          ABRAM FIELD

- JOSEPH HAWKINS exhibitted his claim for taking up a runaway Negro man named Joe belonging to Mr. BENJAMIN SANDERS of HANOVER COUNTY and made oath that he never received any satisfaction for the same which was ordered to be certified
- JOSEPH HAWKINS, Exr. of JOHN HAWKINS deced, Exhibitted a Certificate for his said Father, JOHN HAWKINS taking up a runaway INDIAN man named ROBERT JOHNSON belonging to Mr. THOMAS REVES of PRINCE GEORGE COUNTY and made oath that he never received any satisfaction for the same since the Death of his Father which was ordered to be Certified
- JAMES ROBESON Exhibitted his Claim for taking up a runaway Negro slave that Could or would not tell his Masters name which was committed to this COUNTY GOAL and afterwards sent to the PUBLICK GOAL and he making Oath that he never received any satisfaction for the same, Ordered that the same be certified
- JOHN SCOTT Gent., Exhibitted his claim for taking up two runaway Negro men belonging to the IRON MINE COMPANY at FREDERICKSVILLE in this County and made oath that he never received any satisfaction for the same which was ordered to be certified

- GOODRICH LIGHTFOOT Gent., Assignee of EDWARD WINGFIELD, Exhibitted ye sd WINGFIELDs claim for carrying down JOSEPH MARSH, a Criminal, which was committed by this Court to the PUBLICK GOAL, it being estimated to be one hundred and thirty miles and for summoning the Veuire he having sworn to the Service done, Ordered that the same be certified

- EDWIN HICKMAN Gent. Sheriff exhibitted his claim for carrying down RICHARD CHEEK, a Criminal, which was committed by the Court to the PUBLICK GOAL and for summoning the Veuire &c. he having made Oath to the Service done, Ordered that the same be certified

- No propositions or greivances being presented, Then the Court adjourned

                                                        G. LIGHTFOOT

p.   - At a Court continued & held for Spotsylvania County February ye 4th: 1729
372   Present
          THOMAS CHEW   JOHN SCOTT
          HENRY GOODLOE   ROBERT GREEN   Gentn. Justices

- In the action of Trespass upon the Case brought p BENJAMIN GRAYSON &c. Plt. against CHRISTOPHER WATTERS Defendt., the same is continued to the next Court at ye Plantiffs costs

- In the action of the Case brought p WILLIAM SMITH Gentn. Plt. against EDWARD WINGFIELD Defendt. for ten pounds currant money damage, an order haveing passed agt: the said Defendant in Custody of EDWIN HICKMAN Gentn. Sheriff for what should appear due p a Writt of Enquiry this Court & the Jury being sworn p name GEORGE HOME &c., who after being sworn &c. brought in their verdict in these words Vizt., Wee of the Jury find for the Plantiff Six pounds and eleven pence currant money damage, GEORGE HOME, foreman, which verdict at the Plantiffs motion is admitted to record & Judgment granted for the same with costs and an attorneys fee; It is ordered that the said Defendant in Custody as aforesaid do pay unto the said Plantiff the same alias Exo.

- In the action of Debt brought p JERIMIAH BRONAUGH & ROSE his Wife, Admrs. of JOHN DINWIDDIE deced, Plts. and ABRAHAM FEILD Defendant, On motion of the Plantiff further time is granted him to consider the Defendts. Injunction in Chancery he put in

          - Present ROBERT SLAUGHTER, ABRAHAM FEILD, Gentn. Justices

- The Veiwers appointed to Veiw & mark out the nearest and best way from Collo. HENRY WILLIS MILL in the Fork of RAPAHANNOCK RIVER to GERMANNA, haveing made return of the said Order, which the Court considered & ordered that the same be dismsit

- In the action of Debt brought p JOHN SMITH Plt. against WILLIAM RUSSELL Defendt. for three pounds current money due p Bill, the Defendt. appeared & confessed Judgment for the same with costs and an attorneys fee, It is therefore ordered that the said Defendant do pay unto the said Plantiff the same alias Exo.

- In the action of Debt brought p JAMES BOOTH Plt. against ISAAC MAYFIELD Defendt., at the Plts. motion the same is continued to the next Court at his costs

- In the action of Debt brought p JOSEPH FOX Plt. against GOODRICH LIGHTFOOT Gentn. late Sheriff of Spotsylvania County, Defendt., for one thousand pounds of tobacco damage, issue being joyned & put to Jury p name GEORGE HOME &c. who after being sworn &c. brought in their verdict in these words Vizt. Wee of the Jury find for the Plantiff Eight hundred and thirty pounds of tobacco damage; GEORGE HOME, foreman, which verdict at the Plantiffs motion is admitted to record & Judgment granted for the

same with costs & an attorneys fee, the Defendt. put in & assighned Errors in arrest of
Judgment which were admitted & referred to the next Court for arguement

   - ROBERT TURNER, Deputy Sheriff, made return of several Executions, Vizt.
GEORGE HOMEs Exo. vs. MICHAEL HOLT for 550 pds. of Tobacco & 265 pds. costs (not Executed); JOHN WALLERs Exo. vs. EDWD. WINGFIELD in Custody for 1207 1/2 pds. of tobacco
& 281 costs (not executed); GEORGE HOME Exo. vs. WILLIAM RUSSELL for 1000 pds. of
tobacco & 416: costs (Served)

   - In the action of Debt brought p JAMES TAYLOR Gent., against GEORGE DOWDEY
Defendt. for five hundred & fifty pounds of tobacco due p Bill, the Plantife being dead,
ordered that the suit be dismist

   - JOHN PURVIS acknowledged his Deeds of lease and release for land unto
PHILLIP WATTERS, and ELIZABETH PURVIS, Wife to the said JOHN, acknowledged her
right of Dower of the said land unto the said WATTERS, att whose motion the same were
admitted to record

p.   Spotsylvania County Court 4th of February 1729
373   - On the motion of Mr. JOHN MINOR in behalf of WILLIAM BARTLETT, Overseer of
   the Midle Precincts of the MINE ROAD (that is granted & laid off from
FREDERICKSVILL to RAPAHANOCK RIVER below the HAZEL RUN) and the gang that is
under him setting forth that each other of the precincts are shorter and treble the
number of hands to clear it, especially the first part that is between ye MINE & ye Midle
Precinct does not exceed six miles in length & their precinct is about ten & all to new
clear and many small bridges & long Casways to make; It is therefore ordered that JOHN
KEY with his gang do clear two miles in length more towards & in the Midle Precincts &
that JOHN GRAYSON with his gang do clear one mile lfurther from the BRIDGE built
over the RIVER NY into the Midle precinct of the said road

   - On motion of Dr: WILLIAM BROWN, he was admitted to prove this Accot: against
OWEN JOHNS and the same was ordered to be certified

   - In the action of Trespass brought p JOHN TALIAFERRO JUNR. of CAROLINE
COUNTY Gentn. Plt. against JOHN GRAME Gentn. Defendt. for fifty pounds Sterlin
damage, issue being joyned and referred to this Court for a new tryall & a new Jury p
name GEORGE HOME &c. who after being sworn & heard all evedences &c. brought in
their verdict in these words Vizt. Wee of the Jury find for the Plantife three pounds
seven shillings & eight pence Sterlin damage, GEORGE HOME, foreman; which verdict at
the Plantifes motion was admitted to record, & Judgment granted for the same with costs
& an attorneys fee; The Defendt. on which put in & assighned Errors in arrest of Judgment which were admitted & the same are referred to the next Court for arguement

   - Absent   HENRY GOODLOE
              JOHN SCOTT   Gentn. Justices
              ABRAM FEILD
   - Present   GOODRICH LIGHTFOOT
              WILLIAM BLEDSOE Gentn. Justices
              THOMAS CHEW

   - PHILLIMON CAVENAUGH not makeing returne of the valuation of ye Improvements of his Son, CHARLES CAVENAUGH, on Oath as ye Law enjoyns, the same is referred
to the next Court to be compleated

   - GOODRICH LIGHTFOOT & ROBERT GREEN Gentn. appointed p the Court for lto
agree with some person to build a Bridge over the WILDERNESS RUN, made their return
& the Bond & agreement thay made with Collo. HENRY WILLIS for building the said
Bridge which was ordered to be lodged in the Clerkes Office

- In the action of Debt brought p GEORGE PROCTER Plt. against JOHN YOUNG Defendt., the Plt. failing to appear & prosecute his Suit, ordered that the same be dismist
- In the action of Debt brought p JONATHAN HOOD Plt. against ALEXANDER SPOTSWOOD Esqr., the Defendt. put in a new plea which was admitted (paying two Shillings & six pence cost) and time given the Plantife to consider the same
- In the action of the Case brought p JOHN TALIAFERRO Gentn. Plt. against WILLIAM BICKHAM Defendt., who after haveing leave to plead divers matters put in a plea & time is given the Plt. to consider the same
- In the action of Debt brought p WILLIAM STROTHER Gentn. against JOHN HEWS Defendt., on motion of the Plantife an other plurias capias is granted him
- In the action of Detinue p GEORGE NIX Plt. against EDWARD PRICE Defendt., who put in a plea & time is given the Plantife to consider the same
- In the action of Trespass upon the Case brought p WILLIAM WOODFORD Gentn. against JOHN TALIAFERRO, Gentn., Exr. of ROBERT TALIAFERRO &c. deced, the same is continued over to the next Court

p.   Spotsylvania County Court 4th of February 1729
374   - In the action of Trespass upon the Case brought p GEORGE HOME against CHARLES DUETT JUNR., time is given the Defendant to consider the Plantifes replication
- In the action of Debt brought p CHARLES BURGESS Plt. against OWEN HUMPHRYS Defendt., the Plantife failing to prosecute his suit, ordered that the same be dismist
- In the action of Debt brought p LYONELL LYDE of the City of BRISTOLL, Merchant, Plt. against JOHN TALIAFERRO Gentn., Exr. of ROBERT TALIAFERRO deced, after ye Defendt. had liberty to plead divers matters, he pleaded that he had fully administred & owes nothing & the same is referred to the next Court for tryall
- In the action of Debt brought p OLIVER SEGAR Plt. against ANN JAMES, Admr. of EDWARD SOUTHALL deced, further time is granted to consider the Defendants plea
- In the action of Trespass upon the Case brought p JOHN GRAME Gentn. Attorney of the Honble. ALEXANDER SPOTSWOOD, Plt. against WILLIAM SMALLPEICE Defendt. further time is granted the Plantife to consider the Defendts. plea
- In the action of the Case brought p JOHN WIGLESWORTH Plt. against HENRY GOODLOE Gentn., the Plantifes demurrer being joyned p the Defendant & referred to this Court for arguement, who haveing heard all on each side are of oppinion that the demurrer is good; Therefore Judgment is granted p default for what shall be due p Writ of Enquiry next Court
- In the action of Debt brought p DENNIS LINDSEY Plt. against JOHN DUETT Defendt., special bail being required was granted, afterwards in Custody of the Sheriff he put in a plea, and time is granted the Plantife to consider the same
- In the action of the Case brought p WALTER ANDERSON Plt. against ROBERT EVENS Defendt., for one pound nine Shillings current money, an order haveing passed against the said Defendant in Custody of EDWIN HICKMAN Gentn. Sheriff last Court for the same, & he now failing to appear to answer the suit when called, on motion of the Plantife the said order is confirmed with costs and an attorneys fee; It is therefore ordered that the said Defendt. in Custody of the Sheriff as aforesaid, pay unto the said Plantife the same alias Exo.
- In the action of Covenant brought p WILLIAM SMALLPEICE, Husbandman and Collier, Plt. against JOHN GRAME Gentn. Defendt., on motion of the Defendant he had liberty to mend his plea, paying halfe a Crown costs, & to withdraw his other plea,

afterwards time was given ye Plt. to consider the same

- In the action of Trespass upon the Case brought p ANDREW GLASPE Plt. against RICHARD CHEEK Defendt., a pluria capias is granted the Plantife

- In the Injunction in Chancery brought p EDWARD PRICE against GEORGE HOME further time is given the Defendant to consider the same

- In the action of Debt brought p Our Sovereign Lord the King, Plt. against EDWARD PIGG and CHARLES FILKES PIGG Defendants, whose plea and demurrer being joyned, the same is referred to the next Court for arguement

- In the action of Trespass upon the Case brought p DAVID MITCHELL Plt. against WILLIAM MOORE Defendt., who refuseing to plead, Judgment p Nihil Dicet is granted ye Plantife

- In the action of Debt brought p GEORGE HOME Plt. againt WILLIAM RUSSELL Defendt., at whose motion a special impariance is granted him

- In the action of Debt brought p WILLIAM RUSSELL, Admr. of WILLIAM THOMPSON deced, Plt., against JOHN PENDEGRASS Defendt., on motion of the Plantife special bail is granted & JAMES MACK CULLOW came into Court and assumed to be the Defendts. special bail, afterwards the Defendt. pleaded payment, which issue the Plantife joyned & the same is referred to the next Court for tryall

p.   Spotsylvania County Court 4th of February 1729
375 - In the action of Debt brought p GOODRICH LIGHTFOOT Gentn. Plt. against
     RICHARD CHEEK Defendt. who failing to appear and answer the suit and an alias capias being granted last Court, on motion of the Plantife Attachment is granted him

- On motion of JAMES STROTHER, he is allowed for ten days attendance as he was summoned an evedence for JOHN TALIAFERRO Gentn. against JOHN GRAME Gentn. (he haveing sworn to ye time), It is therefore ordered that the said TALIAFERRO do pay unto the sd STROTHER the same alias Exo.

- On motion of SAMUEL VAUGHN, he is allowed the same order for Ditto vs Ditto

- On motion of JOHN CAMMELL, he is allowed for twelve days attendance as he was summoned an evedence for Ditto vs Ditto, haveing sworn to the time, It is therefore ordered that the said TALIAFERRO do pay the said CAMMELL the same alias Exo.

- Ordered that theCourt be adjourned till tomorrow morning at eight of the Clock
                              G: LIGHTFOOT

- At a Court continued & held for Spotsylvania County February ye 5th 1729
                         Present
        GOODRICH LIGHTFOOT   ROBERT SLAUGHTER
        WILLIAM BLEDSOE   ABRAM FEILD   Gentn. Justices
        JOHN SCOTT

- In the action of the Case brought p RICHARD LONG Plt. against WILLIAM HUTCHESON Defendt., the same is continued at the Plantifes cost

- In the action of Trespass upon the Case brought p JOSEPH ROBERTS Plantife against THOMAS ALLEN Defendt., the same is contined at the Defendants cost

- In the action of Trespass upon the Case brought p JOHN SNELL Plt. against WILLIAM FRAZIER Defendt. for five pounds currant money damage, issue being joyned & put to a JUry for tryall p name GEORGE TILLY &c., who after being sworn &c. brought in their verdict in these words Vizt. Wee of the Jury find for the Plantife two pounds three shillings currant money damage, GEORGE HOME, foreman; which verdict at the Plantifes motion was admitted to record & Judgment granted for the same with costs &

an attorneys fee; It is therefore ordered that the Defendant do pay unto the Plantife
the same alias Exo.

            - JOHN MORGAIN JUNR. & GRACE his Wife, Admx. &c. with ye Will annexed of
JOHN HAWKINGS deced, Plts. against THOMAS CHEW & LARKIN CHEW, Admrs. &c. with the
Will annexed of LARKIN CHEW deced, Defendts., on motion of the Defendants oyer is
granted them of HAWKINGS Letter of Administration

            - It is agreed p this Court with Mr. WILLIAM RUSSELL to give him twelve hun-
dred pounds of tobacco with cask & conveniency to produce the body of EDWARD WING-
FIELD (who broke out of the COUNTY GOAL) att the next Court or deliver him up to the
Sheriff

            - On the petition of WALTER ANDERSON, Ass: of THOMAS MONTEITH, Plt. against
THOMAS CHEW Gentn. Defendt. for four pounds ten Shillings currant money due p Bill,
issue being joyned & submitted to the Court for tryall, who haveing heard all matters
and considered the same, are of oppinon that one pound Eight shillings & ten pence
half penny is due to the Plantife; Therefore ordered that the Defendant do pay the
Plantife the same with costs alias Exo.

            - In the action of Debt brought p THOMAS CARR JUNR. vs. THOMAS CHEW & LAR-
KIN CHEW, Admrs. &c. with the Will annexed of LARKIN CHEW deced, the Defendts.
haveing liberty to plead diverse matters put in a plea & time is given the Plantife to
consider the same

p.   Spotsylvania County Court 5th of February 1729
376   - In the action of the Case brought p MARY HAWKINGS & JOSEPH HAWKINGS,
          Exrs. of JOHN HAWKINGS deced, Plts. against CHARLES GOODALL Defendt. for
three thousand pounds of tobacco damage; issue being joyned and put to a Jury for
tryall p name LARKIN CHEW &c. who after being sworn &c. brought in their verdict in
these words Vizt. Wee of the Jury find for the Plantifes two thousand two hundred &
twenty three pounds tobacco damage, GEORGE HOME, foreman; which verdict at the
Plantifes motion is admitted to record & Judgment granted for the same with costs & an
attorneys fee; The Defendant matter of Law pleaded is referred to the next Court for
arguement

            - In the action of Trespass upon the Case brought p JAMES TAYLOR Gentn.
against THOMAS CHEW & LARKIN CHEW, Admrs. &c. with the Will annexed of LARKING
CHEW Deced, Defendts., the Plantife being dead ordered that the suit be dismist

            - In the action of the Case brought p WILLIAM BARTLETT & WILLIAM BARTLETT
Ass. of SAMUEL BARTLETT, Plt. against HARRY BEVERLEY Gentn., Defendt., who put in a
plea & time given the Plantife to consider the same

            - In the action of Debt brought p ALEXANDER McFARLAND Plt. against THOMAS
CHEW & LARKIN CHEW, Admrs. &c. with the Will annexed, Defendts. the Plantife joyned
the Defendants plea & demurrer & the same is referred to the next Court for tryall &
arguement

            - In the Ejectment brought p JOHN DOE vs. RICHARD ROE, HENRY FITZHUGH Esqr.
entered himself Defendt.. in the stead of RICHARD ROE who thereupon pleaded not
guilty & confessed Lease entry & ouster & the tryall of the issue is referred till the next
Court

            - In the action of Trespass & assault brought p JOHN FOSTER, Deputy Sheriff,
Plantife agt: JOSEPH PARKER, Defendt., the Plantife haveing joyned the Defendants
plea, the tryall thereof is referred to the next Court

            - In the action of the Case brought p JOHN CHAMP Plantife against ROBERT
EVENS Defendt., for eight hundred pounds of tobacco, an order haveing passed against

the said Defendant in Custody of EDWIN HICKMAN Gentn. Sheriff last Court for the same, and the Defendant now failing to appear & answer the suit when called, On motion of the Plantife the said order is confirmed with costs & an attorneys fee; It is therefore ordered that the said Defendt. in Custody as aforesaid do pay the said Plantife the same alias Exo.

    - In the action of the Case brought p ALEXANDER McFARLAND Plantife against JOHN WATTFORD Defendt. who failing to appear & answer the suit when called, on motion of the Plantife an order is granted aginst the said Defendt. and JOSEPH PARKER his security

    - In the action of the Trespass brought p WILLIAM HOLLAWAY Plt. against EDWARD PRICE Defendt. who after haveing liberty to plead diverse matters, put in a plea & time is given Plantife to consider the same

    - In the action of Trespass upon the Case brought p GEORGE TILLY Plantife against JAMES HOLLAWAY Defendant, for six pounds seven Shillings & three pence due p account current money, an order haveing last Court past (on ye non appearance of ye Defendnat) against the said Defendt. and JOHN PARKES his security & he now failing to appear & answer the suit when called, the said Order is confirmed (the Plantife haveing proved his Accot. p his Oath) with costs & an attorneys fee; It is therefore ordered that the said JAMES HOLLAWAY & JOHN PARKES his security do pay unto the said GEORGE TILLY the same alias Exo.

    - On the motion of GOODRICH LIGHTFOOT Gentn. in behalf of himselfe & severall others to have a BRIDLE WAY from the FERRY att GERMANNA unto the Road that comes p Coll. ALEXANDER SPOTSWOODs OLD MILL, is granted & ordered that GEORGE WHEATLEY & the gang of hands under him do clear the same

    - On the Attachment obtained p JAMES GARTON against the Estate of RICHARD CORNELIUS for five hundred pounds of tobacco, the said GARTON failing to appear & prosecute his suit, Ordered that the same be dismist

p.   Spotsylvania County Court 5th of February 1729
377   - THOMAS JERMAIN being called to answer the Presentment of the Grand Jury for suffering his Waggons &c. to pass on the Sabbath Day, produced certificate from under Capt. WILLIAM SMITHs hand of JAMES NICHOLSON, the Driver & his own, that necessity through bad weather &c. occasioned it, Ordered that the said Presentment be dismist he paying costs

    - In the action of Trespass upon the Case brought p THOMAS BENSON Plt. against JOSEPH SMITH Gentn., Defendt. further time is granted the Plantife to consider the Defendts. Injunction in Chancery as he put in

    - In the action of the Case brought p JAMES CANNON Plt. against THOMAS WRIGHT Defendt., the Plantife failing to appear and prosecute his Suit, ordered that the same be dismist

    - In the action of Debt brought p GOODRICH LIGHTFOOT Gentn. Sheriff Plantife, against RICHARD CHEEK Defendt., no Declaration being entered, ordered that the same be dismist

    - In the action of Trespass upon the Case brought p GEORGE TILLY, Merchant, Plt. against FRANCIS KIRKLEY Defendt., who failing to appear and answer the suit, on motion of the Plantife an order is granted against the said Defendt. and ROBERT SLAUGHTER his securety

    - On petition of ANTHONY GOLDSON, he is discharged from being Overseer of the High Way from JOHN KEYS MILL to Capt. JERIMIAH CLOWDERs part of the Road and THOMAS PULLIAM is ordered to serve in his room & all the hands that were under the said

GOLDSON is ordered to serve under & heif the said PULLIAM clear the same

- On motion of HARRY BEVERLEY Gentn. against NICHOLAS HAWKINGS, Overseer of the Road from the COUNTY LINE to the head of GREENS BRANCH for not clearing & keeping his Road in good repair according to Law, it being made appear to the Court, ordered that ahe be fined as the Law directs for the same

- On motion of JOHN SCOTT Gentn., he is allowed for five days attendance as he was summoned an evedence for MARY HAWKINGS & JOSEPH HAWKINGS, Admrs. of JOHN HAWKINGS deced. against CHARLES GOODALL (he haveing sworn to the time) It is therefore ordered that the said Exrs. do pay unto the sd SCOTT the same alias Exo.

- In the action of Trespass upon the Case brought p JAMES McCULLOUGH Plt. against EDWIN HICKMAN Gent., Sheriff of Spotsylvania County Defendt., for two thousand pounds of tobacco damage; the matter of Law pleaded being first argued was adjudged in favour of the Plantife and issue being joyned & put to a Jury for trying the matter of fact p name LARKIN CHEW &c., who after being sworn &c. brought in their verdict in these words Vizt. Wee of the Jury find for the Plantife five hundred pounds of tobacco damage, GEORGE HOME, foreman, which verdict at the Plantifes motion was admitted to record & Judgment granted for the residue with costs and an attorneys fee; It is therefore ordered that the sd Defendt. do pay the said Plantife the same alias Exo.

- In the action of Debt brought p WILLIAM SMITH Gentn., Plantife against FRANCIS ARNOLD Defendt., the Plt. failing to file his Declaration, Ordered that the same be dismist

- Ditto vs MARY HAWKINGS, Widdow: the same order granted

- On the Attachment obtained p WILLIAM MOORE against the Estate of THOMAS GUILLENWATER, the Plantife failing to appear & prosecute his suit, ordered that the same be dismist

- In the action of Trespass upon the Case brought p JOSEPH BROCK Gent., Assee: of WILLIAM SKRINE, Plt. against ANDREW HARRISON Defendt., who failing to appear & answer the suit, on motion of the Plantife an alias Capias is granted him

p.   Spotsylvania County Court 5th of February 1729
378 - In the action of the Case between ROBERT THOMAS Plt. and ABRAHAM BLEDSOE JUNR. Defendt., for fourteen hundred pounds of tobacco damage, there being no appearance, Ordered that the same be dismist

- In the action of Debt between PHILIP SMITH and COMPANY, Merchts., in LONDON Plts. and CHRISTOPHER WATERS Defendt., for ten pounds fourteen Shillings ten pence Farthing sterling due p Protested Bills, Exchange &c., Mr. ZACHARY LEWIS entering himself security for the said Plts. according as the Law directs, the Defendant in Custody of EDWIN HICKMAN Gentn. Sheriff, appeared and confessed Judgment for the same with costs and an attorneys fee; It is therefore ordered that the said Defendt. in Custody as aforesaid do pay the said Plt. the same with costs and an attorneys fee alias Execution

- In the action of Trespass upon the Case between WILLIAM STROTHER Gent. Plt. and ABRAHAM MAYFIELD and LAZARUS TILLY, Defendts., the said Defendts. failing to appear when called and answer the same, an Order againt the aforesd. Defendts. and their securities is granted

- In the action of Debt between THOMAS WITHERBY, Assee. of JOHN MORIS, Plt. and ABRAHAM MAYFIELD Defendt., the same order is granted

- In the action of the Case between RICHARD LONG Plt. and THOMAS DOWDEY Defendt., for four hundred pounds of tobacco damage, there being no appearance, Ordered that tho same be dismist

- On the Scire facias brought by WILLIAM RUSSELL against EDWARD MOSELEY Defendt., the Sheriff having made return not to be found within his Bailiwick. On the Plts. motion an alias Scire facias is granted

- In the petition brought by Docter WILLIAM BROWN Plt. against JOHN GRAME Gent., Attorney of the Honble ALEXANDER SPOTSWOOD Esqr., Defendt., for four pounds nineteen shilings and one penny Currt. money, the Court having heard and considered all matters are of oppinion that nothing is due; Therefore Ordered that the petition be dismist with the costs and an attorneys fee; It is therefore ordered that ye sd Plt. do pay athe said Defendt., his costs and an attorneys fee alias Exo.

- On motion of ROBERT SPOTSWOOD, he was admitted to prove his account against AUGUSTINE SMITH Gentn. and the same was ordered to be certified

- On the Attachment obtained by WILLIAM RUSSELL, Admr. &c. with the Will annexed of WILLIAM THOMPSON deced, Plt. against the Estate of DENNIS MORGAIN for seven hundred and sixty pounds of tobacco due by Accot., the said Admr. &c. having swore that he found ye sd Accot. so stated in ye sd deceased papers, Judgment is granted for the same with costs & an attorneys fee; And JOHN CARDER appearing according to Summonds and on oath declared that he had two hundred and eighty pounds of tobacco and Eight shillings and ten pence current money of the said MORGAINs Estate; Ordered that the said CARDER do deliver the same to the said Admr. &c., and JAMES MORGAIN & WILLIAM RICHESON being summonds on Oath declared they had no Effects of the said MORGAIN in their hands; Therefore Judgment is granted ye Plantiff for the ballance being three hundred and thirty two pounds of tobacco with costs and an attorneys fee; It is therefore ordered that ye sd DENNIS MORGAIN do pay the said RUSSELL, Admr. &c. the same with costs and an attorneys fee alias Execution

- Ordered that the Court be adjourned to the Court in Course
                                        G: LIGHTFOOT

p.   - At a Court held for Spotsylvania County on Tuesday March ye 3d: 1729/30
379   Present
        HENRY WILLIS   THOMAS CHEW
        WILLIAM HANSFORD   HENRY GOODLOE   Gentn. Justices

- On petition of JOSEPH BLOODWORTH to have his marke of Cattle and hoggs recorded, being a slitt & over keel in the right ear and a slitt in the left, is granted & admitted to record

- It is ordered that the rates of Liquors for ORDINARY KEEPERS to seel att be continued the same as they were rated last year

- In complyance with an Act of Assembly Intitled an Act prescribing the Method of Appointing Sheriffs and limitting the time of their continuance in office, and directing their duty therein, the Court have returned a List of three of their members (which are the three oldest in Commission that never yett have been Sheriff) Vizt. HENRY WILLIS, WILLIAM HANSFORD and HENRY GOODLOE Gentn. to the Honble. WILLIAM GOOCH Esqr., his Majties. Lieut: Governor and Commander in Cheife of the Collony and Dominion of Virginia for one of them to be commissionated Sheriff for the ensuing year

- Present WILLIAM JOHNSON, Gentn. Justice

- THOMAS GUY acknowleged his Deeds of Lease and Release for land unto JOHN LATHAM at whose motion the same were admitted to record

- JOHN LATHAM acknowleged his Deeds of Lease and Release for land to WILLIAM RICHESON, and SUSANAH, the Wife of the said JOHN, (after being privately examined) acknowledged her right of Dower of the said Land & at the motion of the sd WILLIAM RICHESON the same were admitted to record

- JOHN LATHAM acknowledged his Deeds of Lease and Release for land unto JOHN BOWMAR, and SUSANAH, the Wife of the said JOHN, (after being privately examined) acknowledged her right of Dower of the said land & at the motion of the said JOHN BOWMAR the same were admitted to record

- JOHN LATAHAM acknowledged his Deeds of Lease and Release for land unto JOHN CHAPMAN, and SUSANAH, the Wife of the said JOHN, (after being privately examined) acknowledged her right of Dower of the said land & at the motion of the said JOHN CHAPMAN the same were admitted to record

- It is ordered that the MAIN ROAD p RAPAHANOCK RIVER be altered & cleared & the same be made and cleared on the bank line of FREDRICKSBURGH TOWN the most convenient way for the good of the said TOWN & that PHILLEMON CAVENAUGH, Overseer with his gang that is under him do alter and cleare the same according to the direction of HENRY WILLIS Gentn.,

- WILLIAM BLANTON acknowledged his Deeds of Lease and Release for land unto THOMAS TURNER and MARGERET BLANTONs Power of Attorney to JOHN WALLER (being first proved p the Oath of RICHARD BLANTON) the said WALLER acknowledged the said MARGERETT right of Dower of the said land to the said TURNER & att the motion of Mr. ZACHARY LEWIS in behalfe of the said TURNER the same were admitted to record

- JOHN GRAYSONs Deeds of Lease and Release unto his Son, AMBROSE GRAYSON, was proved p the Oath of FRANCIS TUNLEY, HENRY ROGERS and JAMES ROY, and SUSANAH GRAYSONs Power of Attorney (being first proved p the Oaths of HENRY ROGERS & FRANCIS TUNLEY) to Mr. ZACHARY LEWIS, the said LEWIS acknowledged her right of Dower of the said Land, and att the motion of the said AMBROSE GRAYSON the same were admitted to record

- AMBROSE GRAYSON acknowledged his Deeds of Lease and Release for land unto HENRY ROGERS, and ALICE the Wife of the said AMBROSE GRAYSON Power of Attorney to JOHN SNELL, being first proved by the Oaths of FRANCIS TUNLEY & JAMES KEY, the said SNELL acknowledged her right of Dower of the said land, And att the motion of the said HENRY ROGERS the same were admitted to record

p.   Spotsylvania County Court 3d of March 1729/30
380   - Collo. HENRY FITZHUGH acknowledged his Deed for land unto WILLIAM WHITE-
HOUS, at whose motion the same were admitted to record

- Collo. HENRY FITZHUGH acknowledged his Deed for land unto JAMES WHEELER, at whose motion the same was admitted to record

- Collo. HENRY FITZHUGH acknowledged his Deed for land unto JOHN THOMPSON SENR. at whose motion the same was admitted to record

- In the action of Trespass upon the Case brought p JAMES JONES Plt. agaisnt EDWARD WINGFIELD Defendt., the Plantife failing to appear & prosecute his suit, Ordered that the same be dismist with costs & an attorneys fee; It is therefore ordered that the said Plantife do pay unto the said Defendt. the same alias Exo.

Present
ROBERT SLAUGHTER   ROBERT GREEN
ABRAHAM FEILD   Gentn. Justices
- In the action of Debt brought p JOHN SMITH Plt. against GEORGE HOME & WIL-LIAM MOORE Defendts., lthe same is continued at the Defendts. costs
- Ditto against WILLIAM MOORE, the same order granted

- In the action of Trespass upon the Case brought p JOHN HOLLADAY Plt. against GEORGE MUSICK Defendt., ordered the suit be dismist, thay being agreed

- In the action of Trespass brought by RICE CURTIS JUNR. Plt. against JOHN SNELL, Defendt., the Plantife failing to appear and prosecute his Suit, ordered that the same be dismist

- In the action of Trespass upon the Case brought p BENJAMIN GRAYSON p JOHN GRAYSON his next Friend, Plt. against CHRISTOPHER WATTERS Defendt., for two pounds seventeen Shillings currant money, the Defendant in Custody of EDWIN HICKMAN Gentn. Sheriff, waved his former plea & submitted the same to the Court which was agreed unto who hearing all matters were of oppinion that one pound Ten Shillings is due on ballance & accordingly Ordered that the said Defendt. (in Custody as aforesaid) do pay unto the said Plantife the same with costs & an attorneys fee alias Exo.

- In the action of Debt between JAMES BOOTH Plt. and ISAAC MAYFIELD Defendt., the same is postponed for two hours

- In the action of Debt brought p LYONELL LYDE of the City of BRISTOLL, Merchant, PLt. against JOHN TALIAFERRO, Gentn, Acting Executor of the last Will & Testament of ROBERT TALIAFERRO deced, for thirty four pounds fourteen Shillings and ten pence Sterlin money: the Defendant p Mr. ZACHARY LEWIS his Attorney appeared & suffered Judgment to pass against the said ROBERT TALIAFERRO deced Estate for the same with costs after his own debt & others of greater Dignity are first paid & satisfied; It is therefore ordered that the said JOHN TALIAFERRO Gentn. Exr. as aforesaid, (if assetts after his Debt & others of greater Dignity are paid and satisfied) do pay unto the said LYDE the same out of the said ROBERT TALIAFERRO deced Estate with costs alias Exo.

- Present WILLIAM BLEDSOE, Gentn. Justice

- In the action of the Case brought p JOHN WIGLESWORTH Plantife against HENRY GOODLOE Gentn. Defendt., for fiveteen pounds currant money damage, Judgment haveing passed last Court for what should appear due p ye Writt of Enquiry this, the Jury being sworn p name JOHN MINOR &c., who after haveing heard all evedences & arguements &c. brought in their verdict Vizt. Wee of the Jury find for the Plantife ten pounds thirteen shillings & eight pence currant money, BENAJ. PORTER, foreman, which verdict at the Plantifes motion is admitted to record and Judgment granted for the same with costs & an attorneys fee; The Defendt. in stay of Judgment assighnd Errors which were argued & overruled p the Court; It is therefore ordered that the said Defendant do pay unto the said Plantife the same alias Exo.

- The petition of ABRAHAM FEILD Gentn. in behalfe of himselfe & severall others to have Mr. FRANCIS THORNTONs former ROLEING HOUSE be again ordered & appointed to be kept for the reception of Tobacco as formerly, was rejected

p.   Spotsylvania County Court 3d of March 1729/30
381   - ZACHARY TAYLOR acknowledged his Deeds of Lease and Release for land unto WILLIAM PHILLIPS at whose motion the same were admitted to record

- ZACHARY TAYLOR acknowledged his Deeds of Lease and Release for land unto GEORGE ANDERSON, at whose motion the same were admitted to record

- WILLIAM PHILLIPS acknowledged his Deeds of Lease and Release for land unto JAMES COWARD, and ANN, the Wife of the said WILLIAM PHILLIPS, Power of Attorney to JOHN WALLER (being first proved p the Oaths of ZACHARY TAYLOR & DAVID PHILLIPS), the said WALLER acknowledged her right of Dower of the said land to the said COWARD at whose motion the said Deeds were admitted to record

- WILLIAM PHILLIPS acknowledged his Deeds of Lease and Release for land unto DAVID PHILLIPS, and ANN, the Wife of the said WILLIAM PHILLIPS, Power of Attorney to JOHN WALLER being first proved by the oaths of ZACHARY TAYLOR & JAMES COWARD, the said WALLER acknowledged her right of Dower of the said Land to the said DAVID PHILLIPS att whose motion the same were admitted to record

- On motion of JOHN ASKUE, he is discharged from being Constable, and ANTHONY FOSTER is ordered to serve in his room, being first sworn before some Magistrate of this County

- On petition of Mrs. JAEL JOHNSON to keep FERRY (as there is one appointed p Act of Assembly to be kept at her Landing over RAPAHANOCK RIVER) the same is granted & ordered that two hands be allowed to keep & tend the said FERRY &c. as the Law directs & that she give bond to perform the same

- On petition of Mr. ZACHARY TAYLOR for liberty to turn and alter the Road that Mr. BENJAMIN CAVE obtained an order of this Court to clear through the SOUTH WEST MOUNTAINS as he have marked in that part of his land where he is going to build about two hundred & fifty yards to come into the MOUNTAIN ROAD a little higer; the same is granted & ordered that he have liberty to turn and alter the same according to petition

- On petition of GEORGE MUSICK to be sett free from paying Publick and County Levys the said petition is rejected

- It is ordered that MICHAEL COOK do serve as Constable for the GERMANS above the CROOKED RUN and in the Fork of the ROBINSON & so to the NORTH RIVER in this County and that he be sworn p some Magistrate of this County Constable accordingly

- In the action of Trespass and Assault brought p JOHN SCOTT Gentn. Plantife against THOMAS CHEW & ROBERT BEVERLEY Defendts., THOMAS CHEW p JOHN MERCER his Attorney & HARRY BEVERLEY Attorney to ROBERT BEVERLEY, put in a plea severally, and time is given the Plantife to consider the same

- In the action of Debt brought p WILLIAM MORTON Plantife against THOMAS CHEW & LARKIN CHEW, Admrs. &c. of LARKIN CHEW deced, Defendts., at whose motion a special Imparlance is granted them

- On petition of THOMAS CHEW & LARKING CHEW in behalfe of the Reverend Mr. THEODOSIUS STAIGE to have his buildings workes & Improvements &c. valued by two or more men upon Oath as the Law directs, with regard to the Account of Expences that he have been att in seating a tract of two thousand acres of land in this County is granted, And ordered that ANDREW HARRISON, JOSEPH HAWKINGS, ROBERT BICKERS, WILLIAM BARTLETT, RICHARD BLANTON and JOHN BUSH or any two of them, being first sworn before one of his Majties. Justices of the Peace for this County, do value the severall kind of Buildings and improvements and on what part of the said land the same are and make return of their proceedings to the next Court

- On petition of THOMAS CHEW to have his buildings workes & Improvements &c. valued p two or more men upon Oath as the Law directs, with regard to account of Expences that he have been att in seating a tract of Four hundred acres of land in this County, is granted, And ordered that ANDREW HARRISON, JOSEPH HAWKINGS, ROBERT BICKERS, WILLIAM BARTLETT, RICHARD BLANTON and JOHN BUSH or any two of them (being first sworn before some Magistrate of this County) do value the severall kind of buildings and Improvements and on what part of the said land the same are and make returne of their proceedings to the next Court

- On petition of RICE CURTIS to have his buildings workes & Improvements &c. valued by two or more men upon Oath as the Law directs, with regard to Account of Expences that he have been at in Seating a tract of Sixteen hundred acres of land in this County, is granted, & ordered that

p.   Spotsylvania County Court 3d of March 1729/30
382   ANDREW HARRISON, JOSEPH HAWKINGS, ROBERT BICKARS, WILLIAM BARTLETT,
      RICHARD BLANTON and JOHN BUSH or any two of them being first sworn before
a Magistrate of this County, do value the severall kind of buildings and Improvements
and of what part of the said land they are and make report of their proceedings to the
next Court

      - On the Attachment obtained p MARY HAWKINGS against the Estate of THOMAS
TYLER, the same is postponed till tomorrow

      - Mr. JOHN CHEW returned a view made p STEPHEN SHARP, JOHN GRAYSON &
PHILLEMON CAVENAUGH of 6000 lb. of Tobacco as they viewed p JOHN TALIAFERRO &
HENRY WILLIS, Gentn. Justices order as the said CHEW tendered on Accot: of Mr. AM-
BROSE MADISON, but not haveing the particular weight & numbers then the same is
referred to the next Court to Lodge the same

      - On petition of NICHOLAS HAWKINGS to be discharged from being Overseer of
the Road from the COUNTY LINE to the head of GREENS BRANCH. he being removed out of
that precinct, is granted and ordered that Mr. RICE CURTIS do serve in his room & all
the tithables that did serve under the sd HAWKINGS do now serve under & help the said
CURTIS clear & keep the said Road in good repair

      - Mr. EDWIN HICKMAN Sheriff made returne of two Executions Vizt.
JOHN ROBINSON vs. PETER GUSTAVUS for 454 lbs. of Tobacco & 353 lbs. tobacco cost;
Executed; JOHN ROBINSON vs THOMAS ALLEN for £ 3...1...4 & 142 lbs. of Toba: & 273 toba
costs, Executed

      - In the action of Trespass & Assault brought p JOHN FOSTER, Deputy Sheriff of
Spotsylvania County, Plt. against JOSEPH PARKER Defendt., the demurrer being joyned
to the matter of Law & fact & the Court after haveing heard all arguements on each side
about ye matter of Law were devided in their oppinions & the same is referred to the
next Court for a fuller Court

      - Mr. WILLIAM RUSSELL according to the Agreement made with the Court,
brought in EDWARD WINGFIELD to the barr & delivered him up unto the Sheriffs
Custody

      - Then the Court adjourned till tomorrow morning att Eight of the Clock

      - At a Court continued & held for Spotsylvania County March ye 4th 1729/30
                              Present
            WILLIAM HANSFORD   WILLIAM JOHNSON
            THOMAS CHEW   ABRAHAM FEILD   Gentn. Justices
            ROBERT SLAUGHTER

      - Ordered that the Clerk do issue to Mr. WILLIAM RUSSELL an order on Collo.
HENRY WILLIS for fourteen hundred & sixty pound of tobacco (for the Service done p
him in fetching back Mr. EDWARD WINGFIELD who had made his escape out of the
COUNTY GOAL) out of the Countys tobacco that is in his hands, and this shall discharge
ye said WILLIS for so much thereof

      - In the action of Debt brought p the Honble. ALEXANDER SPOTSWOOD Esqr. Plt.
against THOMAS JERMAIN &c. special bail being required was granted, afterwards order
passed against the said Defendant & THOMAS BAKER & JOHN ROLLINGS his securetys

      - In the action of Trespass upon the Case brought p THOMAS PHILLIPS Plt.
against ADAM HUBBARD Defendt., at whose motion a special imparlance is granted him

      - In the action of Trespass upon the Case brought p HENRY SNYDER Plantife
against GEORGE HOME Defendt. for two pounds thirteen Shillings & six pence current

money, the Defendt. appeared & confessed Judgment for the same with costs & an attorneys fee; It is therefore ordered that the Defendant do pay unto the said Plantife the same alias Exo.

p.   Spotsylvania County Court 4th of March 1729/30
383   - The Sheriff haveing made returne of GEORGE HOMEs Execution for five hundred & fifty pounds of tobacco and two hundred & sixty five pounds of tobacco costs, served on the body of MICHAEL HOLT, the said HOLT appeared & p Mr. HARRY BEVERLEY, his Attorney, complained of the hardships & unjustness done him p the said HOME whe he had paid & satisfied him for the same before ye Execution was served on him, the Court haveing taken the same into consideration and examined & heard each party found the Complaint to be true (the ballance of six pence excepted) which he paid down in Court; Ordered that the said HOLT be discharged from the said Execution & that the said HOME do pay unto the said HOLT the costs of suit in this Complaint & an attorneys fee alias Exo.

        - In the action of the Case brought p Capt. WILLIAM STROTHER Plt. against PETER CUSTODIE (?) Defendt., for three hundred seventy nine pounds of tobacco, the Defendt. failing to appear and answer the Suit, on the Plantifes motion an order is granted against the said Defendt. and CHARLES BARRETT his securety

        - In the action of Debt brought p JAMES BOOTH Plt. against ISAAC MAYFEILD Defendt., for five thousand pounds of tobacco damage, issue being joyned & put to a Jury for tryall p name JOHN CHEW &c., who after being sworn &c. brought in their verdict in these words Vizt. Wee of the Jury find for the Plantife two thousand one hundred & forty six pounds of tobacco damage, JOHN CHEW, foreman, which verdict at the Plantifes motion was admitted to record & Judgment granted for the same with costs and an attorneys fee; It is therefore ordered that the said Defendt. do pay unto the said Plantife the same alias Exo.

        - On motion of THOMAS NEWTON, he is allowed for six days attendance (haveing sworn to ye time) as he was summoned an evedence for JAMES BOOTH against ISAAC MAYFIELD and for comeing and going twice fifty eight miles and comeing & goeing once forty miles; It is therefore ordered that the said BOOTH do pay the said NEWTON the same alias Exo.

        - On the Attachment obtained p MARY HAWKINGS, Widdow, against the Estate of THOMAS TYLER, THOMAS YATES appeared according to summons & on oath declared that after his discount which was allowed out of his Bill p the Court, their remained due to ye TYLERs Estate seventy six pounds of tobacco which he is ordered to pay to the said HAWKINGS & att her motion the said Attachment is continued to the next Court

        - On motion of PETER MIRTLE, he is allowed for nine days attendance (he haveing sworn to ye time) as he was summoned an evedence for THOMAS YATES against MARY HAWKINGS, Widdow. It is therefore ordered that the said YATES do pay unto the said MIRTLE the same alias Exo.

        - On motion of JOSEPH MERRIOTT, he is allowed for five days attendance (he haveing sworn to ye time) as he was summoned an evedence for ISAAC MAYFIELD against JAMES BOOTH for comeing & goeing three times sixty three miles

        - In the action of Debt brought p WILLIAM RUSSELL, Administrator &c. with the Will annexed of WILLIAM THOMPSON, Plt., against JOHN PENDEGRASS Defendt., for six hundred & sixty pounds of tobacco Cask and conveniency (issue being joyned last Court on payment pleaded after special bail given) and the Defendant now failing to appear to answer the suit when called, Judgment is granted for the same p default with costs & an attorneys fee; It is therefore ordered that the said Defendant do pay unto the said Plantife the same alias Exo.

- Mr. GEORGE HOME not appearing when called as he was summoned on ye Jury, ordered that he be fined for his contempt according to Law, But on his motion & excuse at ye reading of the order, the Court excused him paying costs

- In the action of the Case brought p RICHARD LONG Plt. against WILLIAM HUTCHESON Defendt. for two thousand pounds of tobacco damage; issue being joyned & put to a Jury for tryall p name JOHN CHEW &c., who after being sworn &c. brought in their verdict in these words Vizt. Wee of the Jury find for the Defendt., JOHN CHEW, foreman, which verdict at the Defendts. motion was admitted to record & ordered that the suit be dismist with costs & an attorneys fee, It is therefore ordered that the said Plantife do pay unto the said Defendant his said costs & an attorneys fee alias Exo.

p. Spotsylvania County Court 4th of March 1729/30
384 - JOHN FOSTER, Deputy Sheriff, made returne of two Execution Vizt.
JOSEPH SMITHs vs THOMAS BENSON for twenty Shillings Sterlin & 722 lbs. of Toba: Costs (Executed); SUSANAH LIVINGSTONs vs GEORGE HOME for 314 lbs. of Toba: and 280 lbs. Toba: costs (Executed)

- In the action of Trespass upon the Case brought p JOHN TOWARD Plantife against WILLIAM BAINS, Shewmaker, Defendt., the Sheriff haveing made returne that he could not find him within his Bailiwick, ordered that the suit be dismist

- In the action of Trespass upon the Case brought p HENRY JONES Plantife against WILLIAM RUSSELL Defendt., on motion of the Defendt. a Special Imparlance is granted him

- In the action of Trespass upon the Case brought p GEORGE WOODROFE Plt. against ABRAHAM ABNEY Defendt., at whose motion a special Imparlance is granted, and ordered that THOMAS GRAVES, JOHN WIGLESWORTH & JOHN HOLLADAY or any two of them do some time between this & the next Court veiw and value the Capenders worke done p the said ABNEY for the said WOODROFE & make report of their proceedings to the next Court

- On motion of NICHOLAS HAWKINGS, he is allowed for three days attendance as he was summoned an evedence for RICHARD LONG against WILLIAM HUTCHESON; It is therefore ordered that the said LONG do pay unto the said HAWKINGS the same alias Exo.

- On motion of FRANCIS SMITH, he is allowed for six days attendance as he was summoned an evedence for RICHARD LONG against WILLIAM HUTCHESON, It is therefore ordered that the said LONG do pay unto the said SMITH the same alias Exo.

- In the action of Trespass upon the Case brought p JOHN SNELL Plt. against JOHN WIGLESWORTH Defendt., who failing to appear & answer the suit on motion of the Plantife an order is granted against the said Defendt. and JOHN WILKINGS his securety

- On Attachment obtained by JOHN GRAME, Gentn. Attorney of the Honble. ALEXANDER SPOTSWOOD, against the Estate of JAMES JONES & served in the hands of GOODRICH LIGHTFOOT Gentn., Ordered that the said LIGHTFOOT be summoned to the next Court to give an Accot. of what of the said JONES Estate he had in his hands or possession at the time the said Attachment was served on him

- In the action of Trespass upon the Case brought p JOSEPH ROBERTS Plt. against THOMAS ALLEN Defendt., the same is continued at the Defendants costs

- In the action of Debt brought p JOSEPH FOX Plt. against GOODRICH LIGHTFOOT Gentn. late Sheriff, Defendt., errors being assighnd for the stay of Judgment obtained last Court to be argued this, Likewise the Defendant moved that he might have liberty to prove that the Execution sued for was satisfied and paid p EDWARD WINGFIELD his then Deputy Sheriff, was granted; and it being made appear so to be, Ordered that ye Judgment be reversed and that ye Suit be dismist with costs and an attorneys fee; It is therefore ordered that the said FOX do pay the said LIGHTFOOT the same alias Exo.

- JOHN BOND not appearing to prosecute his petition against THOMAS CHEW and LARKING CHEW, Admrs. &c. with the Will annexed of LARKIN CHEW deced, Ordered that the same be dismist

- In the action of Debt brought p JERIMIAH BRONAUGH & ROSE his Wife, Admrs. &c. with the Will annexed of JOHN DINWIDDIE deced, Plantife, against ABRAHAM FEILD Defendt., the same is continued to the next Court

- On the petition exhibited p Mr. ZACHARY LEWIS in behalfe of Mr. CHARLES CHISWELL & the IRON MINE COMPA. to have the Road of the Midle precincts confirmed where the Overseer varied from the line as the veiwers made report of, the same is rejected

- Ordered that the Court be adjourned to the Court in Course

WILLIAM HANSFORD

p.
385
- At a Court held for Spotsylvania County on Tuesday April the Seventh 1730

Present

GOODRICH LIGHTFOOT   ABRAM FIELD
JOHN SCOTT   ROBERT GREEN   Gentn. Justices

- On petition of JAMES REYNES to have his mark of Cattle and hoggs recorded, which is a crop and Under Keel in each ear, is granted

- On petition of WILLIAM RUSSELL to have his mark of Cattle and hoggs recorded which is a crop and under keel in the left Ear and a half crop in the right ear is granted

- RICHARD GREGORY acknowledged his Deeds of Lease and Release for Land with his Bond for performance of Covenants unto JOHN WHITE; Likewise AGNES GREGORYs Power of Attorney to JOHN WALLER Gentn. (being first proved by the Oaths of THOMAS WHITE and THOMAS CREDERS, the same was admitted to be recorded

- JOHN WHITE acknowledged his Deeds of Lease and Release for land to THOMAS CREDERS & Likewise MARY WHITEs Power of Attorney to JOHN WALLER Gent.(being first proved p the Oaths of RICHARD GREGORY and THOMAS WHITE) the said WALLER acknowledged her right of Dower of the said land to the said CREDERS, at whose motion the same was admitted to be recorded

- Ordered that the Sheriff do summonds a Grand Jury to attend the next Court as the Law prescribes

- On petition of JOHN DURRETT to have the Road as he is Overseer of from JOHN BUSH's to MATAPONY CHURCH devided into two precincts, the same is rejected

- On petition of THOMAS PULLIAM, who was appointed Overseer in the room of ANTHONY GOLDSON of the Road from KEYS MILL PATH to Capt. JERIMIAH CLOWDERs Part of that Road for Tithables to helph him clear & repair the same, is granted, And ordered that ANTHONY GOLDSON, PETERSON PULLIAM, ROBERT TURNER and Collo. MOORE's tithables at his RIDGE QUARTER do help hom clear & keep in good repair the same

- On petition of WILLIAM BARTLETT, Overseer of the Midle Precincts of the MINE ROAD Vizt. from the Ridge between PAMUNKEY and MATTAPONY to the RIVER NY according as it is laid out & marked p the veiwers appointed to be discharged from the same is granted, And ordered that RICHARD BLANTON do serve as Overseer in his room and that all the Male Labouring Tithables that are within four miles of each side of the said Road help him make clear & keep in good repair the same

- On petition of WILLIAM RUSSELL against JOHN PIGG for not building a House in a Workman like manner and to have it veiwed &c., is granted, And ordered that Mr. JOHN FINLESON, FRANCIS MICHALL and WILLIAM PAYTON or any two of them do veiw the same and make return of their proceedings to the next Court

- GEORGE CARR's and CORDELIA CARR's Power of Attorney to JOHN TALIAFERRO Gent. (being first proved p the oath of THOMAS HILL) the said TALIAFERRO acknowledged their Deeds of Lease and Release for a Lott of Town Land in FREDERICKSBURGH to Capt. BENJAMIN BERRYMAN and at the motion of Mr. JOHN MERCER in behalf of the said BERRYMAN, the same was admitted to record

p.   Spotsylvania County Court 7th of April 1730
386   - PHILLEMON CAVENAUGH returned FRANCIS SLAUGHTER, GEORGE HOME and
BENJAMIN TAYLOR report of the proceedings of the valuation of the buildings works & Improvements &c. as required of his Son, CHARLES CAVENAUGHs Tract of four hundred acres of land in the Great Fork of RAPPAHANOCK RIVER in this County, and the said PHILLEMON CAVENAUGH made Oath that none of the said buildings &c. have been before valued in order to save any of the above said land, and at the said CAVENAUGHs motion the same was admitted to record
- On petition of Collo. HENRY WILLIS tohave a Road to his MILL in the Fork of RAPAHANNOCK RIVER from Mr. JOHN FINLESONs ROAD to the upper Inhabitants & from the said Road to his MILL is granted & ordered that JONAS JENKINGS, JOHN ASHLEY & WILLIAM SMITH or any two of them do veiw and lay out the most convenient road according to the said petition & make report of their proceedings to the next Court
- THOMAS CHEW & LARKIN CHEW returned ANDREW HARRISONs & ROBERT BICKERs report of their proceedings of the valuation of the buildings workes & Improvements &c. as required of the Revd. THEODOSIUS STAIGE tract of one thousand acres of land granted p Pattent bearing date the sixteenth day of June Anno. Dom: One thousand seven hundred & twenty seven; the other a purchase of the Revd. THEODOSIUS STAIGE of one ROBERT MARTIN, being by Pattent granted to the said MARTIN dated the thirteenth day of October Anno Dom: one thousand seven hundred & twenty seven in this County, and the said THOMAS CHEW & LARKIN CHEW made Oath as the Law directs that none of the said buildings &c. have been before valued in order to save any of the above said land & at the said CHEWs motion in behalf of the said STAIGE the same were admitted to record
- THOMAS CHEW returned ANDREW HARRISONs and ROBERT BICKERs report of their proceedings & evaluation of the buildings workes & Improvements &c. of his tract of four hundred acres of land in this County and the said THOMAS CHEW made Oath as the Law directs that none of the said buildings &c. have been before valued in order to save any of the above said land & at the said CHEWs motion the same was admitted to record
- THOMAS CHEW in behalf of RICE CURTIS returned ANDREW HARRISONs and ROBERT BICKERs report of their proceedings of the valuation of the buildings workes and Improvements &c. of the said RICE CURTIS tract of sixteen hundred acres of land lying on the SOUTH WEST MOUNTAINS in this County, And the said CHEW in behalf of the said CURTIS made Oath as the Law directs that none of the said buildings have been before valued in order to save any of the said land & that the same might be recorded which was granted
- Present THOMAS CHEW Gentn. Justice
- GEORGE HOME brought before this Court his Servant woman named MARGERETT ROBINSON for haveing a bastard Child & desired an order for one years Service as the Law directs for such offence is granted & Ordered that the said MARGERETT ROBINSON do serve the said GEORGE HOME one whole year after her first indented time is expired; And the said MARGERETT ROBINSON assumeing in open Court to serve her Master, the said HOME, as the Law directs after her indented time & years of service is expired if he

would pay unto the Churchwardens of St. Georges Parrish the five hundred pounds of tobacco or fifty shillings for her fine for the offence committed in being delivered of a bastard Child (which she on Oath declared that one ANDREW JORDEN was the Father of) the said HOME assumed in open Court in her behalf to pay the said fine to the Church-wardens aforementioned which was ordered to be recorded

- ROBERT PATTISON, a Servant boy belonging to Mr. GEORGE HOME, was adjudged to be ten years of age towards his Servitude & paying Publick, County & Parrish levys

- On motion of EDWIN HICKMAN Gentn. Sheriff that whereas Judgment haveing passed & confirmed against him, RICHARD SHARP, FRANCIS MICHAEL & CHARLES MACKORY in August Court last for four thousand pounds of tobacco & cask with costs & an attorneys fee, to have an Attachment granted him against the Estates of the said RICHARD SHARP, FRANCIS MICHAEL and CHARLES MACKORY, the same is granted & ordered that an Attachment do issue

- Absent THOMAS CHEW Gentn. Justice

- THOMAS CHEW and LARKIN CHEW, Administrators with ye Will annexed of LARKIN CHEW Gentn. deced, Exhibitted an Accot: of the said Estate which they desired might be lodged in the Clerks Office, was granted; Likewise the Court then sitting on motion of the said Adminsitrators adjudged & allowed ten shillings p Cent for tobacco towards settling the said Accot: and Ten p Cent for trouble & Charge of Administration and fiveteen p cent between Sterlin & Currency

- Present THOMAS CHEW Gentn. Justice

p. Spotsylvania County Court 7th of April 1730
387 - GEORGE HOME acknowledged his Deeds of Lease and Release for land unto JOHN FINLESON, at whose motion the same were admitted to record

- On petition of Mr. GEORGE HOME, Surveyor, that the Surveyors Book belonging to this County now in the hands of AUGUSTINE SMITH Gentn., late Surveyor, may be delivered him as the Law directs, It is ordered that the said AUGUSTINE SMITH Gentn. be summoned to answer the said petition & deliver the same

- On petition of DENNIS GRADY in order to prove his rights to take up land accor-ding to the Royall Charter made oath that he came into this Countrey and brought MARY his Wife with him and that this is the first time of his proveing the said Impor-tations; Whereupon Certificates is ordered to be granted him of Rights to take up One hundred acres of land

- On petition of SUSANNAH LIVINGSTON to keep FERRY at FREDERICKSBURG the same is granted and Ordered that two hands be allowed to keep and tend the same, she having entered into bond &c. as the Law directs

- On the Scire facias brought by WILLIAM RUSSELL agaisnt EDWARD MOSELEY Defendt. for three hundred pounds of tobacco and two hundred and fifty seven pounds of tobacco costs due p Judgment, the same Judgment is renewed against the sd Defendt. with costs and an attorneys fee; It is therefore ordered that the said MOSELEY do pay the said RUSSELL the said sum of three hundred pounds of tobacco and two hundred and fifty seven pounds of Tobo: with costs & an attorneys fee alias Exo.

- Mr. ROBERT TURNER, Deputy Sheriff, made return of several Executions Vizt. WILLIAM RUSSELL Exo. vs JOHN PENDERGRASS for 660 lbs. Tobo: & 324 lbs Tobo. costs, Executed; WM. RUSSELLs Exo. vs ANDREW GLASPE FOR 250 Tobo & 344 Tobo. costs, Exe-cuted; JOSEPH SMITH Gentn., Exo. vs. WM. RUSSELL for 20/ Sterlin & 903 1/2 Tobo costs, Executed; SAMUEL WRIGHT Exo. vs WM. RUSSELL for 213 1/2 pounds of Tobo. Cost, Executed; JOHN SMITH Exo. vs WM. RUSSELL for L 3...0...0 Currt. money & 311 Tobo: costs, Executed; BENJAMIN GRAYSON &c. Exo. vs. DANLL. HUFF and JNO. SHARP for 500 lbs. of

Tobo: & 252 Tobo costs not Executed; CHARLES CHISWELL Gentn. vs GOODRICH LIGHTFOOT for £ 4...15...0 1/2 current money and 263 pounds of tobacco costs, Executed; ALEXANDER SPOTSWOOD Esqr. vs. ANDREW HARRISON for 997 lbs. tobo. costs Not executed. ZACHARY LEWIS vs JAMES McCOLLOUGH for £ 1...10...0 Currt. money & 100 lbs. Tobo: costs, Executed

- Mr. JOHN FOSTER Deputy Sheriff returned the Courts order wherein they appointed RICE CURTIS to be Overseer of the Road from the COUNTY LINE to the head of GREENS BRANCH and Informed the Court that the said CURTIS would not accept the said Order to put it in Execution (which he declared on Oath) Ordered that the said CURTIS be fined Twenty Shillings Current money for his Contempt and that he be continued Overseer of the said Road

- On motion of sundry people to this Court setting for that Whereas their being but one Coroner at present in the County, severall processes cannot be served where that Coroner and the Sheriff are both concerned desiring them to make application to his Honble. the Governor to have more Coroners commissionated; It is ordered that the Clerk do wait on his Honble. the Governor to desire him to issue more Coroners Commissions as to him shall seem meet for this County

p.   Spotsylvania County Court 7th of April 1730
388
- In the action of Trespass upon the Case brought by JOHN SUTTON Plt. against RICHARD LONG Defendt., for one thousand pounds of tobacco, Cask and conveniency, the Sheriff having made return (not Executed by reason he kept of with a Staff) on motion of ye sd Plantiff an Attachment is granted against the sd Defendt. in the hands of Mr. WILLIAM RUSSELL

- Ordered that the Court be adjourned till the Court in Course
                          G: LIGHTFOOT

- At a Court held for Spotsylvania County on Tuesday May the fifth 1730
                          Present
        GOODRICH LIGHTFOOT   JOHN SCOTT
        THOMAS CHEW   ABRAM FIELD   Gentlemen Justices

- On petition of THOMAS JACKSON he is discharged from being Constable and ordered that BENJAMIN PORTER do serve as Constable in his room he being first sworn before of his Majties Justices for this County
- On petition of CHRISTOPHER PARLOW to be sett free from paying of Publick and County Levys (he being old and lame in his Limbs &c.) is granted
- On petition of CYRACUS FLESHMAN to be sett free from paying of Publick and County levys (he being very lame, Antient and unable to work) is granted for this year only
- On petition of CHRISTOPHER ZIMMERMAN to have his mark of Cattle and hoggs recorded which is a crop on the left ear and a half crop on the right, is granted
- HENRY WILLIS and JOHN WALLER Gentn. two of the Trustees of FREDERICKSBURGH TOWN in this County acknowledged their Deeds of Lease and Release for a Lot of the sd Town Land unto Collo. WILLIAM TODD, and at the motion of JOHN WALLER JUNR. in behalf of the said TODD the same were admitted to record
- Ditto acknowledged their Deeds of Lease and Release for a Lott of the sd Town Land unto Collo. DAVID BRAY and at the motion of JOHN WALLER JUNR., in the said BRAYs behalfe, the same was admitted to be recorded

- Ditto acknowledged their Deeds of Lease and Release for a Lot of Town Land to Mr. SUSANNA LIVINGSTON & at the motion of JOHN WALLER JUNR., in the said SUSANNA's Behalf the same were admitted to be recorded

- RICHARD BLANTON is appointed Overseer of the precincts of the MINE ROAD in the room of WILLIAM BARTLETT And ordered that ye sd BLANTON with the tithables which served upon the said Road under the former Overseer, keep in good repair the same as the said BARTLETT have already cleared

p.   Spotsylvania County Court 5th of May 1730
389   - Present HENRY WILLIS, ROBERT GREEN Gentn. Justices
- ISAAC NORMAN acknowledged his Deeds of Lease and Release for Land unto JOHN REED and FRANCES NORMAN, the Wife of the said ISAAC (after being privately Examined) acknowledged her right of Dower of the said land unto ye sd REED at whose motion the same was admitted to be recorded

- On petition of EDWARD PRICE he is discharged from being Constable and ordered that JOHN MARTIN do serve as Constable in his room; he being first sworn before a Magistrate of this County

- On petiton of THOMAS CRETHERS, JOSEPH ROBERTS & GEORGE MUSICK to be released from service on five roads, is granted, and ordered that they only serve on the MINE ROAD that goes from Capt. JERIMIAH CLOWDERs ROLING ROAD to the CHURCH

- On motion of Mr. ZACHARY LEWIS in behalf of Mr. RICE CURTIS to be discharged from being Overseer of the Road from the COUNTY LINE to the head of GREENS BRANCH as NICHOLAS HAWKINS was formerly Overseer, is granted and ordered that ROBERT HUTCHESON do serve in his room (he being freed and exempted from all other Roads) and all the Tithables that served under the former Overseer do help the sd HUTCHESON clear and keep in good repair the same

- Mr. RICE CURTIS appeared and moved that the Court would remaitt the Five of Twenty Shillings as he was last Court for not accepting of the Order of Court and clearing the Road as he was appointed Overseer of and that they would be pleased to put some other person in his room he giving the Court satisfactory reasons; It is ordered that he be discharged from being Overseer of the said Road and that Collo. HENRY WILLIS be desired to wait on his Honble. the Governor to interceed to have the said fine remitted

- JOHN VENTON is made Overseer of the Road Vizt. from the FALLS to the WILDERNESS BRIDGE and Ordered that all the Tithables that served under the former Overseer of the said Road do help the said VENTON clear and keep in good repair the same
                    - Absent ROBERT GREEN, Gentn. Justice
- WILLIAM ROSIER alias Ward Servant of Mr. ROBERT GREEN being brought before this Barr p his said Master for absenting himself from his said Masters Service Eighteen days and Eighteen Shillings and one penny half penny current money charges paid and expended in recovering of him again, and five hundred pounds of tobacco for taking him up (as p Accot: exhibitted) and the said Servant having nothing to say in his Defence, Ordered that he serve for the same according to Law after his first indented time be expired

- PAUL FOUNTAIN, Servant of Mr. ROBERT GREEN, the same order granted for ten days absence and for eight shillings and one penny half penny current money charges paid & expended &c.
                    - Present ROBERT GREEN Gent. Justice

p.   <u>Spotsylvania County Court 5th of May 1730</u>

390   - The Grand Jury according to summonds appear when called and being sworn for the body of this County p name JOSEPH HAWKINS, JOHN SNELL, RICHARD BLANTON, WILLIAM RICHESON, JOHN DURRITT, SAMUEL HENSLEY, JOHN BOND, JOHN HADOCKS, JOHN ASHER, JOHN CHRISTOPHER, BENJAMIN PORTER, JOHN SMITH, CHARLES FILKS PIGG, WILLIAM MOORE, JOHN RUCKER, NICHOLAS HAWKINS and RICHARD SHARP and having received their charge retired

- The the Court adjourned till three of the Clock in the afternoon

- At a Court held for the Proof of Publick Claims in Spotsylvania County on Tuesday May ye 5th 1730   Present

HENRY WILLIS   ABRAM FIELD
JOHN SCOTT   ROBERT GREEN   Gentlemen Justices

- WALTER BUTLER exhibitted his claim for taking up a runaway Negro man that could or would not tell his Masters name, which was commited to this COUNTY GOAL and he making Oath that he never received any satisfaction for the same, ordered that the same be certified

- JOHN SMITH exhibitted his Claim for taking up a runaway white Servant belonging to ELIZABETH PITTS in ESSEX COUNTY and the said Certificate being not granted regularly, the same rejected

- JOHN SMITH exhibitted his Claim for taking up a runaway Negro man named Sam belonging to Collo. HENRY WILLIS and he making oath that he never received any satisfaction for the same, ordered that the same be certified

- Present WILLIAM BLEDSOE Gent. Justice

- WILLIAM BECKHAM Exhibitted his Claim for taking up a runaway Negro man named Harry belonging to Capt. WILLIAM BEVERLEY of ESSEX COUNTY and he making Oath that he took up the runaway p Mr. MOSLEY BATTALEYs Plantation near the FALLS of the RAPPAHANOCK, which is above ten miles from the sd Runaways Quarter, and never received any satisfaction for the same, ordered that the same be certified

- ZACHARY TAYLOR Exhibitted his Claim for going as a Guard to WILLIAMSBURGH with a Criminall named JOSEPH MARSH (he being summoned by the Sheriff) having made Oath to the Service done, Ordered that the same be certified

- WILLIAM SMALLPEACE exhibitted his Claim for taking up a runaway Negro man named Ben belonging to Collo. ALEXANDER SPOTSWOOD and he making Oath that he never received any satisfaction for the same, Ordered that the same be certified

- At a Court held for receiving Propositions and Greivances in Spotsylvania County on Tuesday May the Fifth Anno Dom 1730

Present

HENRY WILLIS   JOHN SCOTT
WILLIAM BLEDSOE   ABRAM FIELD   Gentlemen Justices
                  ROBERT GREEN

- ZACHARY LEWIS in behalf of himself and severall others exhibitted a Proposition for to have the Court days of the adjacent Countys STAFFORD and CAROLINE altered which was admitted and ordered to be Certified

- HENRY FIELD in behalf of himself and several others exhibitted a Proposition for not ringing and confining the hoggs in the (   ) County which was admitted and ordered to be certified

p.   Spotsylvania County Court for Receiving Propositions & Greivances Fifth of
391   May 1730

- HENRY FIELD in behalf of himself and severall others exhibitted a Proposition
for deviding this County which was admitted and ordered to be Certified

- Ditto in behalf of himself and severall others exhbitted a Proposition for deviding the Parish and refunding and paying back the Upper Inhabitants rateable part
of Twenty eight thousand five hundred pounds of Tobacco raised to pay for a GLEBE
which was admitted and ordered to be certified

- Ditto in behalf of himself and several others Exhibitted a Proposition for
Erecting a new County on the South side of PATOWMACK RIVER and the Western side of
the GREAT RIDGE of MOUNTAINS and that the Inhabitants that goes to Seat there might
be levy free which was admitted and ordered to be certified

- Ditto in behalf of himself and severall others exhibitted a greivance about the
demand of the Lessee of NORTHERN NECK ESTATE to claim right to the land in Fork of
RAPPAHANOCK RIVER in this County, which was admitted and ordered to be certified

- MOSLEY BATTALEY in behalf of himself and severall others exhibitted a Proposition for the MINERS to pay their levys in their respective Countys and be prepayd by
the Publick which was admitted and ordered to be certified

- No more Propositions or Greivances being Exhibitted and Proclamation being
made the Court rose up

- At a Court held for Spotsylvania County p Adjournment May the Fifth Anno
Dom 1730   Present
            HENRY WILLIS
            WILLIAM BLEDSOE   JOHN SCOTT   Gentlemen Justices
            THOMAS CHEW

- The Grand Jury returned and brought in the following Presentments Vizt.
We do present HENRY CURTIS for swering three oaths within two months last past;
We also present JOHN PHILIPS and DYANAH his House Keeper for Living in Adultry
                                        JOSEPH HAWKINS, foreman

- Ordered that the several people presented be summoned to the next Court to
answer the same

- Ordered that the Court be adjourned till to Morrow morning NIne of the Clock
                                        HENRY WILLIS

p.   - At a Court continued & held for Spotsylvania County May the Sixth Anno Dom:
392   1730   Present
            GOODRICH LIGHTFOOT   ABRAM FIELD
            JOHN SCOTT   ROBERT GREEN   Gentlemen Justices

- A Proclamation for Repealing of the Acts of Assembly past in 1705 Entitled the
Act of Limitation &c. was proclaimed in Court and returned p the Sheriff and ordered to
be lodged in the Clerks Office

- Mr. JOHN FOSTER, Deputy Sheriff made return of severall Executions Vizt.
JAMES BOOTHs Exo. vs ISAAC MAYFIELD for 2146 lbs. Tobo: & 1305 lbs. Tobo. Costs, not
Executed; JOHN SNELLs Exo. vs. WM. FRAZIER for £ 2...3... Currt. & 376 Tobo: costs, Exe-
cuted; WALTER ANDERSONs Exo. vs. ROBERT EVANS for £ 1...9 Curt. & 278 Tobo: costs, not
Executed

- EDWIN HICKMAN, Gentn. Sheriff acquainted the Court that Collo. HENRY WILLIS denyed the paying of the Courts Order to WILLIAM RUSSELL for fourteen hundred and sixty pounds of tobacco out of the County Tobacco that is lodged in his hands; Ordered that he be summoned to give his reasons for so doing to the next Court, Otherwise they shall order the said Tobaccos to be taken out of his hands

- JOHN SCOTT Gent. is appointed and desired to take the List of Tithables from PLENTIFULL RIVER across to ye WILDERNESS RUN so along the RIVER RAPPADAN to the Extent of the County towards the Mountains this present year

- ROBERT GREEN Gent. is appointed and desired to take the List of Tithables in the Fork between RAPPAHANOCK and RAPPADAN RIVERs this present year

- AMBROSE GRAYSON Gent. is appointed and desired to take the List of Tithables from the RIVER PO to RAPPAHANOCK RIVER across the County to the WILDERNESS RUN this present year

- JOSEPH BROCK Gent. is appointed and desired to take the List of Tithables between the RIVER TA and the RIVER PO across the County and up to the WILDERNESS RUN this present year

- HENRY GOODLOE Gent. is appointed and desired to take the List of Tithables betweenthe RIVERs TA and NORTHANNA from the COUNTY LINE to PLENTIFULL RIVER this present year

- CHRISTOPHER SMITH acknowledged his Deeds of Lease and Release for land unto PATISON PULLIAM and at the motion of JOHN HOLLADAY in behalf of the said PULLIAM the same were admitted to record

- ROBERT TURNER, Deputy Sheriff, made return of severall Executions Vizt. WM. RUSSELL Admr. of THOMPSON Exo. vs ANDREW GLASPE for 250 lbs. Tobo: & 394 lbs. Tobo Costs, Executed; Collo. ALEXANDER SPOTSWOODs Exo. vs THOMAS DAVIS for L 10...9...5 Sterlin & 569 lbs. Tobo. costs, not Executed; Ditto"s Exo. vs. ANDREW HARRISON for 997 lbs. Tobo Costs, not Executed; WM. MOORE's Exo vs WM. RUSSELL for 830 lbs. tobo; and 255 lbs. Tobo. Costs, not Executed; BENJAMIN GRAYSONs &c. Exo. vs DANIEL HUFF and JOHN SHARP for 500 lbs. Tobo. & 232 lbs. Tobo. costs, not executed

p.   Spotsylvania County Court 6th of May 1730
393   RICHARD HARRALL's Exo. vs. DAVID WILLIAMS for 300 lbs. Tobo: and a436 lbs. Tobo: Costs, not Executed

- In the action of Trespass upon the Case between JOSEPH ROBERTS Plt. and THOMAS ALLEN Defendt., for three pounds current money damage, Issue being joyned and put to a Jury for tryall p name JOHN HOLLADAY &c., who after being sworn & heard all Evedences on each side &c. brought in their verdict in these words; We of the Jury find for the PLant: Nineteen Shillings and nine pence current money, ROBT. SPOTSWOOD, foreman; which verdict at the Plts. motion was admitted to record and Judgment granted for the same with Costs and an attorneys fee; It is therefore ordered that the said Defendt. do pay the Plt. the same with costs and an attorneys fee alias Exo.

          - Present WILLIAM BLEDSOE
          - Absent GOODRICH LIGHTFOOT   Gentn. Justices

- In the action of Debt between ALEXANDER McFARLAND Plt. and THOMAS CHEW and LARKIN CHEW, Admrs. &c. with the Will annexed of LARKING CHEW Gent. late Sheriff of Spotsylvania County, Defendts. for twenty pounds Sterling damage, the Defendts. demurrer being joyned and the matter of Law being first argued was by the Court adjudged not goot and a Jury being summoned and Sworn to try the matter of fact p name ROBERT SPOTSWOOD &c. who after haveing heard all arguements &c. brought in their verdict in these words Vizt. Wee of the Jury find for the Plantiff Eleven pounds fifteen Shillings and six pence Sterling and three hundred and seventeen pounds of tobacco damage; but no assetts, ROBERT SPOTSWOOD, foreman; which verdict at the Plantiffs motion was admitted to record and Judgment granted when assetts with costs from which Judgment ye sd Admrs. &c. appealed, which was granted them, they having entered into bond to answer and prosecute the same before the Honble. the General Court next on the eighth day thereof

        - Absent WILLIAM BLEDSOE
        - Present HENRY WILLIS   Gentn. Justices

    - In the action of Trespass between JOHN TALIAFERRO Gent. Plt. and JOHN GRAME Defendt., continued at Defendts. costs

    - In the action of Debt between JONATHAN HOOD Plt. and Collo. ALEXANDER SPOTSWOOD Defendt., time is given ye sd Defendant to consider the Plts. replication

    - In the action of the Case between JOHN TALIAFERRO Gent. Plt. and WILLIAM BECKHAM Defendt., issue joyned and referred for tryall

    - In the action of Debt between WILLIAM STROTHER Gent. Plt. and JOHN HEWS Defendt., the Sheriff having returned the plurias capias as not Executed, on Motion of ye sd Plantiff the plurias capias is continued

    - In the action of Detinue between GEORGE NIX Plantiff and EDWARD PRICE Defendt., time given the Defendt. to consider the Plts. replication

    - In the action of Trespass upon the Case between WILLIAM WOODFORD Gent. Plt. and JOHN TALIAFERRO, Gent., Exr. &c. of ROBERT TALIAFERRO deced, Defendt., for thirty five pounds Currt. money, there being no prosecution, ordered that the same be dismist

    - In the action of Trespass upon the Case between GEORGE HOME Plt. and CHARLES DUETT JUNR. Defendt., issue joyned and referred for tryall

    - In the action of Debt between OLIVER SEGAR Plt. and ANN JAMES, Admr. &c. of EDWARD SOUTHALL deced, Defendt. time is given to consider the Plts. replication

p.   Spotsylvania County Court 6th of May 1730

394   - In the action of the Case between JOHN GRAME, Atto. of the Honble. ALEXANDER SPOTSWOOD Esqr. Plt. and WILLIAM SMALLPEACE Defendt., continued at the Plts. costs

    - In the action of Debt between DENNIS LINDSEY Plt. and JOHN DUETT Defendt., for Eight hundred & thirty pounds of tobacco due by Bill, there being no prosecution, and being agreed, ordered that the same be dismist

    - In the action of Trespass upon the Case between ANDREW GLASPE Plt. and RICHARD CHEEK Defendt. for six hundred pounds of Tobo: damage, and the Sheriff having made return on the plurias capias not executed, and there being no prosecution ordered that the same be dismist

    - In the Injunction in Chancery brought by EDWARD PRICE vs. GEORGE HOME, time is given to consider ye Respondants answer as he gave in on Oath

    - In the action of Covenant between WILLIAM SMALPEACE Plt. and JOHN GRAME Gent., Defendt., time is given to consider the Defendants new plea

    - In the action of Debt between Our Sovereign Lord King George Plt. and EDWARD PIGG and CHARLES FILKES PIGG Defendts. for twenty pounds current money due by bond, the Demurrer of ye sd Defendts. being joyned and put to the Court for arguement, who having heard all on each side, are of oppinion that the said Demurrer is good, Therefore it is ordered that the suit be dismist

    - On motion of JOHN HOLLADAY, he is allowed for two days attendance as he was summoned an evedence for THOMAS ALLEN against JOSEPH ROBERTS; It is therefore ordered that the said ALLEN do pay the said HOLLADAY the same with costs alias Execution

- In the action of Trespass upon the Case between DAVID MITCHELL Plt. and WILLIAM MOORE Defendt., time to cnsider the Defendts. plea and demurrer is granted

- In the action of Debt between GEORGE HOME Plt. and WILLIAM RUSSELL Defendt., issue joyned and referred to the next Court for tryall

- In the action of Debt between GOODRICH LIGHTFOOT Gent., (otherwise called GOODRICH LIGHTFOOT of the Parish of St. George and County of Spotsylvania Gent. Sheriff) Plt. and RICHARD CHEEK otherwise called RICHARD CHEEK of the same Parish and County Gent., Defendt., for one thousand pounds Sterling due by bond, there being no prosecution, ordered that the said Suit be dismist

- In the action of Debt between JOHN MORGAN and GRACE his Wife, Admx. &c. with ye Will annexed of JOHN HAWKINS deced, Plts. and THOMAS CHEW & LARKIN CHEW, Admrs. &c. with ye Will annexed of LARKIN CHEW deced, Defendts., further oyer is granted

                    - Present THOMAS CHEW Gent. Justice

- In the action of Trespass upon the Case between MARY HAWKINS and JOSEPH HAWKINS, Exrs. of the last Will and Testament of JOHN HAWKINS deced, Plts. and CHARLES GOODALL Defendt. for three thousand pounds of tobacco damage, the Defendts. plea of abatement being joyned and put to the Court for arguements, who haveing heard all on each side, are of oppinion that the said plea is not good; Therefore Judgment according to the Jurys Verdict is granted, which was two thousand two hundred and twenty three pounds of tobacco damage with costs & an attorneys fee from which Judgment the said Defendt. by his Attorney appealed, which was granted. Mr. ZACHARY LEWIS in behalfe of the said Defendt. having entred into bond and acknowledged the same in Court to answer and prosecute the same before the Honble. the Generall Court next on the eighth day thereof

p.   Spotsylvania County Court 6th of May 1730
395   - On motion of THOMAS CRETHERS, he is allowed for four days attendance as he was summoned an Evedence for THOMAS ALLEN against JOSEPH ROBERTS (he having sworn to the time), It is therefore ordered that the said ALLEN do pay the sd CRETHERS the same with costs alias Exo.

- In persuance to an Order of the President and Council held at the Capitoll May the 6th: 1727 on the Petition of JAMES TAYLOR, Surveyor of Spotsylvania County, for appointing Commissioners to mee and joyn with the Commissioners that shall be appointed p HANOVER COUNTY for ascertaining the bounds and settleing the said Dividing Line between the two Countys and to direct the Surveyors to mark out the same persuant to the Directions of the Act of Assembly &c. The Court in obedience thereto did in November Court anno 1727 appoint JERIMIAH CLOWDER, LARKIN CHEW and JOHN TALIAFERRO Gentn. to meet ye sd Commissioners to execute the said Order, but some of those Gentlemen being dead or not in the Commission of the peace, On motion of Mr. ZACHARY TAYLOR, GOODRICH LIGHTFOOT, THOMAS CHEW and JOHN SCOTT Gentn. are desired and appointed to meet the said Gentlemen Commissioners p HANOVER COUNTY Court to lay of the said Countys Line. the Eighteenth day of this Instant May or the next fair day

- In the action of Debt between THOMAS CARR JUNR. Plt. and THOMAS CHEW & LARKIN CHEW, Admrs. &c. with the Will annexed of LARKIN CHEW deced, Defendts., time to consider the Plts. replication is granted

- In the action of Trespass upon the Case between WILLIAM BARTLETT & WM. BARTLETT, Ass: of SAMLL. BARTLETT, Plt. and HARRY BEVERLEY Gent. Defendt., the Plt. joyned ye Defendts. demurrer and referred to the next Court for arguement

- In the action of the Case between ALEXANDER McFARLAND Plt. and JOHN WATFORD Defendt., for two pounds ten Shillings current money damage, the same being agreed, ordered that ye suit be dismist

- In the action of Trespass between WILLIAM HOLLAWAY Plt. and EDWARD PRICE Defendt., time to consider the Plts. replication is granted

- On the Injunction in Chancery between JOSEPH SMITH Gent. and THOMAS BENSON Defendt., time is given to consider the Respondts. answer (which ye sd Respondt. gave in on Oath)

- In the action of Trespass upon the Case between GEORGE TILLY Plt. and FRANCIS KIRKLEY Defendt., the Defendt. failing to appear and answer the same, an order is confirmed for what shall appear due p Writt of Enquiry against him and his security next Court

- In the action of Trespass upon the Case between JOSEPH BROCK Gent. Ass: of WM. SKRINE, Plt. and ANDREW HARRISON Defendt., ye sd Defendt. failing to appear and answer ye suit, an order against him and his security is granted

- In the action of Trespass upon the Case between WILLIAM STROTHER Gent. Plt. and ABRAHAM MAYFIELD and LAZARUS TILLY Defendts. the said Defendts. failing to appear and answer the same, an Order is confirmed against the sd Defendts. and their securitys for what shall appear due p Writ of Inquiry next Court

- In the Ejectione Firme between JOHN DOE Plt. and HENRY FITZHUGH Esqr. Defendt., THOMAS SMITH, Lessor, the Plantife not prosecuting, at the Defendts. motion he is nonsuited, And it is considered by the Court that the Defendant recover against the Lessor of the Plt. damages according to Law, together with one attorneys fee and costs alias Exo.

p. **Spotsylvania County Court 6th of May 1730**
396
- In the action of Debt between THOMAS WOTHERBY, Assignee of JOHN MORIS, Plt. and ABRAHAM MAYFIELD Defendt. for seven hundred pounds of tobacco Cask Convenient due p Bill, the said Defendt. failing to appear when called to answer the same And an Order having last Court passed against him and WILLIAM BECKHAM his security for the same, now is confirmed for the said sum of Seven hundred pounds of Tobo. Cask and conveniency against ye sd Defendt. & his security with costs & an attorneys fee: It is therefore ordered that the sd Defendt. and his security do pay the Plt. the same with costs and an attorneys fee alias Exo.

- In the action of Debt between WILLIAM STROTHER Gent. Plt. and EDWARD PRICE Defendt. for twenty pounds Sterling damage, there being no further prosection, Ordered that the same be dismist

- In the action of Trespass upon the Case between WILLIAM STROTHER Gent. Plt. and GEORGE HOME Defendt., oyer granted

- Ditto vs Ditto the same order granted

- Ditto against WILLIAM HANSFORD Gent. Defendt. who failing to appear and answer when called, an order against the sd Defendt. and Sheriff is granted

- In the action of Trespass upon the Case between JAMES NICOLL, Mercht., Plt. and ANDREW HARRISON Defendt., the said Defendt. failing to appear and answer, an order against him and his security is granted

- In the action of Trespass upon the Case between FRANCIS SLAUGHTER Plt. and WILLIAM RUSSELL Defendt. for ten pounds Sterling damage, there being no further prosecution, ordered that the same be dismist

- In the action of Debt between THOMAS PULLIAM Plt. and GEORGE GOING Defendt., for Six hundred pounds of tobacco, there being no declaration filed, ordered that the same be dismist

- Ditto against Ditto the same order
- In the action of Trespass upon the Case between ROBERT THOMAS Plt. and ABRAHAM BLEDSOE JUNR. Defendt., for eight hundred pounds of Tobacco damage, the Sheriff having made return that the Writt came too late to his hands to execute, and there being no further prosecution, ordered that the same be dismist
- In the action of Trespass upon the Case between WILLIAM TAPP Plt. and JOHN ELSON Defendt., for ten pounds current money damage, there being no Declaration filed, ordered that the same be dismist
- In the action of Trespass upon the Case between ROBERT JONES Plt. and PETER CASSITY Defendt. for ten pounds current money Damage, there being no further prosecution, ordered that the same be dismist
- In the action of Trespass upon the Case between GEORGE MERIDATH Plt. and WILLIAM SMITH Gent. Defendt. for two pounds Eleven shillings and six pence current money due by Accot: the Sheriff having returned a Copy Left, on motion of ye sd Plantiff an Attachment against ye sd Defendts. Estate is granted
- On the Attachment obtained by Capt. WILLIAM STROTHER against the Estate of EDWARD PRICE for twenty nine hundred and eight pounds of Tobacco in three casks convenient in a ROLEING HOUSE &c. due by Bill, Judgment for the same with costs and an attorneys fee is granted and the Sheriff haveing returned served on Severall things Vizt. Eleven head of Cattle and one hhd. of Tobacco and one bulk of Stript Tobo: about twelve hundred and a parcell of Tobo: not stript about three hundred, Ordered that the said Sheriff do sell the said things as the Law directs to satisfie and pay the above said Judgment and costs &c. land make return of his proceedings to the next Court

p   Spotsylvania County Court 6th of May 1730
397   - In the action of Trespass upon the Case between JAMES DYER Plt. and EDWARD WINGFIELD Deft., the said Defendt. failing to appear and answer the same, an Order against him & his security is granted
- In the action of Trespass upon the Case between THOMAS CRETHERS Plt. and JOHN CUDDIN Defendt., for three pounds current money damage, the same being agreed, ordered that the suit be dismist
- Ditto against WILLIAM CUDDIN, the same order
- In the action of Trespass upon the Case between WILLIAM HACKNEY Plt. and GOODRICH LIGHTFOOT Gent. Defendt. for four pounds current money damage, the suit being agreed, ordered that the same be dismsit
- In the action of Trespass upon the Case between JOHN DAVISON Plt. and PHILIP SANDERS Defendt., the Sheriff returned not executed, On motion of the sd Plt. an alias capias is granted
- In the action of Trespass upon the Case between HENRY RAINES Plt. and WILLIAM MOORE Defendt. for twelve hundred pounds of tobacco damage, the same being agreed, Ordered that the suit be dismist
- In the action of Trespass upon the Case between JOSEPH KEATON Plt. and JOHN SNOW Defendt., the said Defendt. failing to appear and answer the same, an order against him & his security is granted
- In the action of Trespass upon the Case between MICHAEL GUINNEY Plt. and WILLIAM CANON Defendt. the said Defendt. failing to appear and answer when called, an order against him and his security is granted
- In the action of Debt between ROGER QUARLES, Assignee of WILLIAM HIGGENS, Plt. and JOHN SMITH Defendt., for one pound ten Shillings current money due by Bill, the suit being agreed, ordered that the same be dismist

- On the petition of EDWARD PRICE, Ass. of RICHARD CHEEK, against GEORGE HOME Defendt., for Eight hundred and Ninty nine pounds of Tobo: the Sheriff having made return that the Summonds came too late to his hands to be executed, Ordered that the same be dismist

- On the Scire facias brought by JOHN SUTTON Plt. against HENRY DILLEN and HENRY BERRY Defendts., the Sheriff having returned not Executed, on the said Plts. motion an alias Scire facias is granted

- In the action of Trespass upon the Case between JOHN SAVAGE Plt. and BENJAMIN WHITE Defendt., the Sheriff having returned not executed, On motion of ye sd Plt. an alias Capias is granted

- In the action of Trespass upon the Case between GEORGE HARRISON Plt. and EDWARD WINGFIELD Defendt., an order against the sd Defendt. and Sheriff is granted

- In the action of Trespass Assault and Battary between JOHN STEVENS Plt. and ABRAHAM BLEDSOE JUNR., Defendt. a special Imparlance is granted

- In the action of Debt between EDWARD FRANKLYN Plt. and HENRY CURTIS Defendt. who failing to appear and answer the same, an order against him and his security is granted

p.   Spotsylvania County Court 6th of May 1730
398
- On the Attachment obtained by JAEL JOHNSON, Widow, Admx. of all and singular ye goods chattels & Credits of RICHARD JOHNSON deced, against the Estate of JAMES BOOTH, the Sheriff having returned served in the hands of ISAAC MAYFIELD, Ordered that he be summoned to Declare what of ye sd BOOTHs Estate he had in his hands when the said Attachment was served on him, to the next Court

- On the Attachment obtained by WILLIAM RUSSELL, Admr. &c. of WILLIAM THOMPSON deced, against the Estate of THOMAS ROPLEY for four hundred and seventy seven pounds of Tobacco due by Accot: there being no further prosecution, Ordered that the same be dismist

- In the action of Trespass upon the Case between DAVID WAUGH Plt. and THOMAS MALONEY Defendt., who failing to appear and answer when called, an order against him and his security is granted

- In the action of Trespass upon the Case between JOHN MERCER Plt. and Ditto Defendt., no prosecution, dismist

- In the action of Trespass upon the Case between RICHARD SHARP Plt. and JOHN ELSON Defendt., who failing to appear and the Sheriff having returned not executed, On motion of ye sd Plt. an alias capias is granted

- In the action of Trespass upon the Case between CHARLES CHISWELL Gent. Plt. and JOHN PERCY MASON Defendt., for thirty pounds Sterling damage, there being no further prosecution, Ordered that the same be dismist

- In the action of Trespass upon the Case between NICHOLAS HAWKINS PLt. and WILLIAM RICE Defendt., for six hundred and twenty pounds of Tobacco damage, the same order is granted

- On the Attachment obtained by JOHN WALLER against the Estate of WILLIAM SMITH Gent., the Sheriff having returned served in the hands of RICHARD PARSLOW, Ordered that the said PARSLOW be summoned to declare what of ye sd SMITHs Estate he had in his hands when the said Attachment was served on him the next Court

- Present WM. BLEDSOE, Gent. Justice

- On the petition of EDWARD PRICE, Assignee of RICHARD CHEEK, against GEORGE HOME Defendt., for eight hundred & ninety nine pounds of Tobacco due by Bill, the Defendt. pleased owe nothing which ye Plt. joyned and referred to the Court for tryall, who having heard all evedence and arguements on each side, are of oppinion and accordingly order that Judgment be granted for the same with costs and an attorneys fee; It is therefore ordered that the sd Defendt. do pay the said Plt. the same alias Execution

   - In the action of Debt between THOMAS CHEW and LARKIN CHEW, Admrs. with ye Will annexed of LARKIN CHEW Gent. Sheriff of Spotsylvania County deced, Plts. and WILLIAM RUSSELL and JAMES McCOLLOUGH Defendts., (special bail being required is granted)afterwards an order passed against the said Defendts and their security

   - In the action of Trespass and Assault between JOHN SCOTT Gent. Plt. and THOMAS CHEW and ROBERT BEVERLEY Gent., Defendts. issue joyned and referred to the next Court for tryall

   - In the action of Debt between WILLIAM STROTHER Gent. Plt. and RICHARD CHEEK and EDWARD PRICE Defendts., for three thousand five hundred and fifty seven pounds of tobacco in four hogsheads (in Mrs. JAEL JOHNSONs ROLING HOUSE) due by Bill, EDWARD PRICE one of the Defendts. came into Court and suffered Judgment to pass for the same with costs and an attorneys fee against the said Defendants and JAMES WILLIAMS, JOHN PRICE, EDWARD PRICE JUNR. and JOHN FOSTER their securitys; It is therefore ordered that the said Defendants and their securitys

p.   Spotsylvania County Court 6th of May 1730
399   do pay the said Plantiff the same with costs and an attorneys fee alias Execution
      - Ordered that the Court be adjourned till the Court in Course
                                     G. LIGHTFOOT

         - At a Court held for Spotsylvania County on Tuesday June the Second Anno Dom
1730   Present
         GOODRICH LIGHTFOOT   ROBERT SLATTER
         THOMAS CHEW   WILLIAM JOHNSON   Gentlemen Justices
         JOSEPH BROCK   ABRAM. FIELD
                                     ROBERT GREEN

   - On petition of JOHN WALLER JUNR. for to have his mark of Cattle and hoggs recorded which is Vizt. a Swallow Fork in the left ear and a flower de Luce in the right ear is granted

   - In the action of Trespass and assault between JOHN FOSTER, Deputy Sheriff, of Spotsylvania County Plt. and JOSEPH PARKER Defendt., for fifty pounds Sterling damage, the issue on the Defendts. demurrer being first argued, And the Court haveing heard all on each side, are of oppinion that the same is not good; And a Jury being summonded and sworn to try the matter of fact p name JOHN CHEW &c., who after having heard all evedences &c. brought in their Verdict Vizt. We of the Jury find that JOHN FOSTER Plantiff then Deputy Sheriff on ye Sixteenth day of Augst. in ye year of our Lord One thousand seven hundred and twenty nine, did repair to ye House of JOSEPH PARKER Deft. to serve an execution on JOHN CAMMEL then in the House of the said Defendt., And we also find that ye sd Deft. did thrust ye sd Plt. backwards out of his House and hindred him the Sheriff for some time serving the execution aforesaid, And we also find yt: afterwards the Deft. gave ye Plt. leave to serve ye Execution in his House; Therefore we find for the Plt. Forty Shillings Sterling damage if the Law is for him and if the Law is for the Deft. we find for him, JOHN CHEW, foreman; which was admitted to be recorded And time granted to argue the same to the next Court

   - MARY, the Wife of GEORGE PROCTER, came into Court (after being privately examined) & acknowledged her right of Dower to JOSEPH PARKER of a parcel of land

containing eighty six acres, which her said Husband sold to ye sd PARKER at whose
motion the same was admitted to be recorded

- EDWIN HICKMAN Gent. produced his Honble. WILLIAM GOOCH Esqr. Leiut.
Governor & Comander in Chief of Virginia Commission to be Sheriff of this County this
ensueing year, which being read, and he having entered into bond with JOSEPH BROCK
and JOHN WALLER Gentn., his Securitys, and acknowledged the same, Likewise having
taken the Oath & signed the Test, was sworn SHERIFF accordingly

- EDWIN HICKMAN, Gent. Sheriff, presented ROBERT TURNER and JOHN FOSTER, to
be his Deputy Sheriffs for this County, and they having taken the Oaths & signed the
Test, was sworn accordingly

- EDWIN HICKMAN Gent. Sheriff made Exception against the Sufficiency of the
COUNTY PRISON to this Court, who have referred the consideration of the same some
time before the (blurred) of the Court

p.   Spotsylvania County Court 2d of June 1730
400   - On petition of ADAM HANIE for to be free and Exempt from paying Publick and
          County Levies, he being antient and unable to work &c., the same is granted
- In the action of Debt between WILLIAM MORTON Plt. and THOMAS CHEW and
LARKIN CHEW, Admrs. with the Will annexed of LARKIN CHEW deced, Defendts. the same
is continued at the Defendts. costs

- In the action of Debt between the Honble. ALEXANDER SPOTSWOOD Esqr. Plt. and
THOMAS JARMAN &c. Defendt. (special bail being required is granted) oyer in Custody is
granted

- Ordered that ABRAHAM ABNEY be fined Five Shillings or fifty pounds of
tobacco for being & appearing in Court Drunk and pay costs

- ELIZABETH, the Wife of GEORGE HOME, came into open Court and after being
privately examined, acknowledged her right of Dower to Mr. JOHN FINLESON of a parcell
of land containing Four hundred acres, which her said Husband sold the said FINLESON,
And at the motion of JOHN WALLER JUNR. in behalf of ye sd FINELSON the same was
admitted to record

- Ordered that the Sheriff do take ABRAHAM ABNEY into Custody and there to
remain till he enter into bond of Forty pounds Sterling with good security for his appearance before the next Court to answer for his misbehaviour and breaking of the
STOCKS

- On the Attachment obtained by MARY HAWKINS, Widow, against the Estate of
THOMAS TYLER, the same is continued

- In the action of Trespass upon the Case between THOMAS PHILIPS Plt. and
ADAM HUBARD Defendt. the same is continued at the Defendts. costs

- In the action of the Case between Capt. WILLIAM STROTHER Plt. and PETER
CUSTODIE Defendt., an order having last Court passed against him & his security, the
same is confirmed for what shall appear due p Writ of Enquiry next Court

- In the action of Trespass upon the Case between HENRY JONES Plt. and WIL-
LIAM RUSSELL Defendt., Judgment p Nihil Dicit granted

- In the action of Trespass upon the Case between JOHN SNELL Plt. and JOHN
WIGLESWORTH Defendt., an order having last Court passed against him, ye sd Defendt. &
his security, the same is confirmed for what shall appear due p Writ of Enquiry next
Court

- On the motion of GEORGE HOME, he is allowed for five days attendance as he was
summoned an evedence for JOSEPH PARKER against JOHN FOSTER, Deputy Sheriff, (he
having sworn to ye time), It is therefore ordered that ye sd PARKER do pay the said
HOME the same with costs alias Exo.

- In the action of Trespass upon the Case between GEORGE WOODROOF Plt. and ABRAHAM ABNEY Defendt., the Veiwers appointed having returned their report which was ordered to be Lodged in the papers, And the Defendt. afterwards pleaded which the said Plt. replyed on & issue joyned & referred for tryall to the next Court

- On motion of JOHN GRAYSON JUNR. he is allowed for five days attendance as he was summoned an evedence for JOHN FOSTER, Deputy Sheriff, against JOSEPH PARKER (he having sworn to the time), It is therefore ordered that the said FOSTER do pay the said GRAYSON the same with costs alias Exo.

p. Spotsylvania County Court 2d of June 1730
401
- WILLIAM SMITH Gent. Power of Attorney to his Wife, ELIZABETH SMITH, and RICHARD PHILLIPS was in open Court proved p the Oaths of JOSEPH FOX & THOMAS BALARD SMITH, And on motion of the said PHILIPS in behalf of himself and Mrs. ELIZABETH SMITH, the same was ordered to be certified

- THOMAS CHEW Gentn. acknowledged his Deeds of Lease and Release for Land unto LARKIN CHEW, at whose motion the same was admitted to record

- On motion of Mr. JAMES HORSNALE, he is allowed for five days attendance as he was summoned an evedence for JOHN FOSTER, Deputy Sheriff, against JOSEPH PARKER (he having sworn to the time); It is therefore ordered that the said FOSTER do pay the said HORSNALE the same with costs alias Exo.

- ROBERT TURNER, Deputy Sheriff, made return of severall Executions Vizt. WILLIAM MOOR vs WILLIAM RUSSELL for 830 lbs. Tobo. & 255 lbs. of Tobo. Costs, not Executed; RICHARD HARRALL vs DAVID WILLIAMS for 300 lbs. Tobo: & 436 lbs. Tobo. costs, not Executed; JOHN WALLER vs. EDWARD WINGFIELD for 1207 1/2 Tobo: 7 381 Tobo. costs, not Executed

- JOHN FOSTER, Deputy Sheriff, made return of Several Executions, Vizt. EDWARD PRICE Ass: of RICH. CHEEK, vs. GEORGE HOME for 899 lbs. Tobo & 265 lbs. Tobo. costs, Executed; ALEXANDER SPOTSWOOD Esqr. vs ANDREW HARRISON for 997 lbs. Tobo: costs, Executed

- JOHN FOSTER, Deputy Sheriff, having brought before this Court GEORGE HOME by the vertue of an Execution which EDWARD PRICE, Ass: of RICHARD CHEEK, obtained against him for eight hundred & ninty nine pounds of Tobacco and two hundred and sixty five pounds of Tobacco costs; Ordered that the Sheriff do commit the said HOME to PRISON till he have paid and satisfied the same

- Ordered that the Court be adjourned till the Court in Course
W: HANSFORD

- At a Court held for Spotsylvania County on Tuesday July the Seventh Anno
Dom. 1730   Present
GOODRICH LIGHTFOOT   ROBERT SLAUGHTER
WILLIAM BLEDSOE   JOHN SCOTT   Gentlemen Justices

- Mr. NATHANIEL CLAYBOURNE, Surveyor, made return of a List of Surveys made by him in his precincts in this County which was admitted and ordered to be recorded

- Mr. GEORGE HOME, Surveyor, the same Order

- JOHN WALLER JUNR. acknowledged his Deeds of Lease and Release for land unto JOHN WALLER SENR. at whose motion the same were admitted to be recorded

- ROBERT DUDLEY, Deputy Sheriff of CAROLINE COUNTY, made return of the following Executions Vizt.: WILLIAM HUTCHESON vs RICHARD LONG for 211 1/2 pounds of Tobo: costs., not Executed

p.   Spotsylvania County Court, 7th day of July 1730

402   - JOSEPH COOPER acknowledged his Deeds of Lease and Release for land unto Mr.
        FRANCIS THORNTON and BARBARY, the Wife of ye sd JOSEPH, after being private-
ly examined, acknowledged her right of Dower of the said land unto ye said FRANCIS at
whose motion the same was admitted to record

        - On motion of THOMAS STANTON to have his Servant boy named JAMES
McKENNEY adjudged was granted and he was adjudged to be nine years of age towards
Servitude and paying of levys

        - JOHN McKENNY belonging to ROGER ABBOTT is adjudged to Eleven years of age,
the same order

        - JOHN GRANT, belonging to GEORGE WHEATLEY, is adjudged to Twelve years of
age, the same order

        - FENLEY McCOUCHMAN belonging to Ditto is adjudged to Ten years of age, the
same order

        - WILLIAM BARON belonging to WILLIAM DUNCOMB is adjudged to seven years
of age, the same order

        - DUNCOMB GRANT belonging to Ditto is adjudged to ten years of age, the same
order

        - In the action of Debt between JOHN SMITH Plt. and GEORGE HOME and WILLIAM
MOOR Defendts., for eighteen hundred and forty five pounds of Tobacco in three casks
convenient due p Obligation: Issue being joyned and referred to a Jury for tryall p
name JOHN MINOR &c., who after being sworn and heard all evedences &c., brought in
their verdict Vizt. We of the Jury find for the Plantiff eighteen hundred and forty five
pounds of Tobacco to be paid in three hhds. Convenient according to the tenor of the
Obligation, JOHN MINOR, foreman, which verdict at the Plts. motion was admitted to
record and Judgment granted for the same with costs and an attorneys fee; It is therefore ordered that the said Defendts. do pay the Plt. the same with costs and an attorneys
fee alias Execution

        - JOHN WIGLESWORTH and RICHARD BLANTON came into Court and gave bond for
Keeping the MINE BRIDGE that the said WIGLESWORTH built and finished over the
RIVER PO in good repair seven years according to agreement made with Mr. CHARLES
CHISWELL, which was ordered to be lodged in the Clerks Office

        - On motion of Mr. WILLIAM RUSSELL in behalf of the Honble. ALEXANDER
SPOTSWOOD Esqr. to have his Son, JOHN SPOTSWOODs age recorded towards ye payment of
Levys, who was four years of age the Twenty sixth day of December last the same was
granted

        - On petition of BENJAMIN PORTER to be discharged from being Overseer of the
MOUNTAIN ROAD, the same is rejected till such time he hath made the said Road in good
repair

        - JOHN ROBERTS and FRANCIS KIRKLEY acknowledged their Deeds of Lease and
Release for land unto ROGER OXFORD, and ELIZABETH ROBERTS and MARGRETT KIRKLEY
(after being privately examined) acknowledged their right of Dower of the said land
unto ye sd OXFORD, at whose motion the same was admitted to record

        - In the action of Debt between JOHN SMITH Plt. and WILLIAM MOOR Defendt., for
one thousand one hundred and fifty pounds of tobacco in one Cask convenient, the
Issue being joyned being waved p consent, the Defendt. came into Court and confessed
Judgment for the same with costs and an attorneys fee; It is therefore ordered that the
said Defendant do pay the aforesaid Plt. the same alias Exo.

        - On petition of Mrs. SUSANNAH LIVINGSTON to have her ORDINARY LICENCE
renewed, is granted, she giving bond &c. and pay the Governours dues

p.   Spotsylvania County Court 7th of July 1730
403   - On motion of GEORGE COLLEY, he is allowed for five days attendance and for
       forty miles coming and going four times as he was summoned an evedence for
WILLIAM MOORE against JOHN SMITH (he having sworn to the time); It's ordered that
the said MOORE pay ye sd COLLEY the same with costs alias Exo.
       - WILLIAM RUSSELL Gent. in behalf of the Honble. ALEXANDER SPOTSWOOD Esqr.
brought to this barr JOHN HAMBLETON, a Servt. man belonging to ye sd SPOTSWOOD, for
absenting himself from his said Masters Service three years & from the fifteenth of
March last past, And the said Servant having nothing to say in his defence, Ordered
that he Serve for the same according to Law and Likewise for the Charges of recovery
that shall be made appear after his first indented time expired
       - ABRAHAM ABNEY appearing to answer his Misbehaviour to the last Court and
breaking of the STOCKS &c., he having acknowledged his fault and promising his good
behaviour for the future, Ordered that the said Complaint be dismist, he paying costs
and all fees
       - In the action of the Case between JOHN TALIAFERRO Gent. of CAROLINE COUNTY
Plt. and WILLIAM BECKHAM Defendt. for four hundred & ninty pounds of tobacco
damage, the demurrer joyned being first argued, the Court are of oppinion that the
Demurrer is not good; And a Jury being Impaneled and sworn to try the matter of fact p
name JOHN MINOR &c., who after having heard all evedence and arguements brought
in their verdict Vizt. We of the Jury find for the Defendant, JOHN MINOR, foreman;
which verdict at the said Defendts. motion was admitted to record, And ordered that the
suit be dismist with costs and an attorneys fee; It is therefore ordered that ye sd Plt. pay
the said Defendt. the same with costs and an attorneys fee alias Exo.
       - On the Attachment obtained p JOHN GRAME Gent., Attorney to the Honble
ALEXANDER SPOTSWOOD Esqr. agst. the Estate of JAMES JONES, GOODRICH LIGHTFOOT Gent.
appearing according to summons and on oath declared that he had no estate or did owe
the sd Defendt. any thing; Ordered that ye said Attachment be continued
       - JOHN CHEW to return the Marks, Weights & Numbers of tobacco veived on a
Tender made to Mr. AMBROSE MADISON, the same is continued to the next Court
       - On the petition of WILLIAM RUSSELL vs JOHN PIGG to have a House viewed as
the said PIGG built for the said RUSSELL, the viewers according to order of the last Court
vived the said House and made returne of their report Vizt. Persuant to the within
order, Wee the Subscribers mett at the House of the within mentioned WILLIAM RUS-
SELL to view the House built by JOHN PIGG. Wee find the said House insufficient work &
not built workman like. Given under our hands this day & year above written
                April ye 25th 1730   JOHN FINLESON
                                               FRANCIS MICHAEL
                                               WM. PAYTON
       - On the petition of HENRY WILLIS Gentn. about a Road to his MILL, the same is
continued to the next Court, he being on the Assembly
       - On the action of Debt between JERIMIAH BRONAUGH JUNR. & ROSE his Wife,
Admx. with the Will annexed of JOHN DINWIDDIE Gentn., late of KING GEORGE COUNTY,
deced &c. the Respondt. put in an answer in Chancery and time is given the Complaints.
to consider the same
       - On petition of GEORGE HOME, Surveyor, vs AUGUSTINE SMITH Gentn., late Sur-
veyor for the delivery of the County Book, the same is continued to the next Court, he
being on the Assembly

p.   Spotsylvania County Court 7th of July 1730

404   - On the action of Trespass upon the Case brought p JOHN SUTTON Plt. against
RICHARD LONG Defendt., for fiveteen pounds currant money, the Sheriff having
attached (on the non appearance of the said Defendt.) all the Estate of the sd LONGs in
the the hands of WILLIAM RUSSELL who appeared in Court and on oath declared that he
had thirteen hundred & fiveteen pounds of tobacco in his hands when the attachment
was served. Afterwards Judgment was granted the Plantife for what shall appear due p
Writt of Enquiry next Court against the said Defendant

- HENRY CURTIS being called to answer the Presentment of the Grand Jury for
swearing three Oaths & failing to appear when called, ordered that he be fined for the
same according to Law

- JOHN PHILLIPS & DIANAH, his Housekeeper, being called to appear and answer
ye Presentment of the Grand Jury for liveing in Adultery & failing to appear according
to summonds, Ordered that thay be attached to answer the same next Court

- On petition of SAMUEL HENSLEY, he is allowed for ten days attendance as he
was summoned an Evedence for JOHN TALIAFERRO Gentn. vs WILLIAM BICKHAM; It is
therefore ordered that the said TALIAFERRO do pay the said HENSLEY the same alias Exo.

- JOHN FOSTER, Deputy Sheriff, made returne of the following Executions, Vizt.
PHILLIP SMITH & COMPA. vs WATTERS & CAMMELL for L 5...19...3 Sterlin and 278 lbs
Toba: cost, Executed; JOHN CHAMP vs ROBERT EVENS for 800 lbs. Toba: & 278 lbs. Toba:
costs, not Executed

- On motion of Mr. ZACHARY LEWIS in behalfe of Mr. CHARLES BARRETT, an
Attachment is granted against the Estate of PETER CASSITY, the said BARRETT being
security for the said CASSITY in an action brought against him p WILLIAM STROTHER
for three hundred & seventy nine pounds of Tobacco for which Judgment was granted
against the said CASSITY and BARRETT his security for what shall appear due p Writt of
Enquiry next Court

- Ordered that the Court be adjourned till the Court in Course
                                    G: LIGHTFOOT

- At a Court held for Spotsylvania County August the fourth Anno Dom 1730
                            Present
            HENRY WILLIS   HENRY GOODLOE
            GOODRICH LIGHTFOOT   JOSEPH BROCK   Gentlemen Justices
            WILLIAM HANSFORD   ROBERT SLAUGHTER
            THOMAS CHEW   ROBERT GREEN

- On petition of THOMAS MARRY, Infant, to have Liberty to choose his Guardian,
is granted, who appointed and desired Mr. RICE CURTIS might be the same which was
admitted, the said RICE CURTIS having entered into bond as the Law directs

- ANDREW GORDEN, a Servant of Mr. GEORGE HOME, being brought before the
Court p his said Master for absenting himself from his said Masters Service five months
and ten days being from the twentieth day of February to the thirtieth day of July last
past and for eight pounds five shillings current money charges paid and expended in
recovering and taking him up (as p Accot: exhibitted) and the said Servant having
nothing to say in his Defence, Ordered that he serve for the same according to Law
after his first Indented time be expired

- On petition of ROBERT HUTCHERSON, Overseer of the Road from the COUNTY
LINE to the head of GREENS BRANCH, which said road crosses ye BRIDGE over ye RIVER
NY; And that sd BRIDGE being so out of repair that his gang was not able to mend &

repair the same, neither is there any Timber to do it, the same rejected till the new Law
be sent to this Court & Ordered that ye Clerk do issue out an order in the mean time to
him for all the tithables yt. served under NICHOLAS HAWKINS former Overseer to help
ye sd HUTCHESON

P.   Spotsylvania County Court 4th of August 1730
405   repair the said BRIDGE
         - The Honble. ALEXANDER SPOTSWOOD Esqr. produced the Honble. EDWARD
         CARTERET and EDWARD HARRISON Esqrs. his Majesties Post Masters Generall of
all his Majestys Dominion in Europe, Africa and America Commission to be sole and only
Deputy Post Master Generall of all his Majestys Province and Dominions in North
America and the West Indies and having taken the Oaths as the Law enjoyns and signed
the Test, On his motion the said Commission was admitted to record
         - The Honble ALEXANDER SPOTSWOOD Esqr. produced a Power of Attorney p him
made to Mr. WILLIAM RUSSELL and desired that the same might be certified which was
granted
         - HENRY WILLIS Gent. produced his Honble. WILLIAM GOOCH Esqr. Lieut. Gover-
nour and Commander in Cheif of Virginia Commission to be Leiut. Collonell of this
County, Likewise his said Honble. Commission for being Coroner, having taken the
Oaths as the Law directs & signed the Test was sworn accordingly
         - GOODRICH LIGHTFOOT Gent. produced his Honble. WILLIAM GOOCH Esqr. Lieut.
Governor and Command in Cheif of Virginia Commission to be Coroner of this County,
having taken the Oath and signed the Test, as the Law enjoyns, was sworn accordingly
         - On petition of JOHN HADDOX to have his mark of Cattle and hoggs which is a
Crop and slitt in the right ear and hole in ye Left, admitted to record is granted
         - DAVID CAVE acknowledged his Deeds of Lease and Release for Land unto
DANIEL COOK at whose motion the same was admitted to record
         - In the action of Trespass upon the Case between GEORGE HOME Plt. and
CHARLES DUETT JUNR. Defendt. for five hundred pounds of tobacco due p Accot:, issue
being joyned and put to a Jury for tryall p name LARKIN CHEW &c. who after being
sworn and heard all Evedence &c. brought in their verdict Vizt. Wee of the Jury find
for the Defendant LARKIN CHEW, foreman; which verdict at the Defendants motion is
admitted to record and Ordered that the Suit be dismist with costs and an attorneys fee; It
is therefore ordered that the Plt. do pay the said Defendant the same alias Execution
         - On motion of FRANCIS MICHALL, he is allowed for three days attendance as he
was summoned an Evedence for CHARLES DUETT JUNR. at ye suit of GEORGE HOME (he
having sworn to the time), It is therefore ordered that the said DUETT do pay the said
MICHALL the same with Costs alias Exo.
         - ROBERT CAVE, the same order granted
         - On the Attachment obtained by EDWIN HICKMAN Gent. Sheriff against the Es-
tate of RICHARD SHARP, FRANCIS MICHALL and CHARLES MACKOREY for four thousand
pounds of tobacco and cask and two hundred & ninety five pounds of tobacco costs due p
Judgment &c., the sd Attachment being returned served on the goods of the said SHARP
and MICHALL and the proceedings of the said Attachment bieng no legally brought,
Ordered that the same be dismist with costs & an attorneys fee; It is therefore ordered
that ye sd Plt. do pay the said Defendts, the same alias Exo.
         - Present WILLIAM BLEDSOE Gent. Justice
         - In the action of Trespass upon ye Case between GEORGE TILLY, Mercht., Plt. and
FRANCIS KIRKLEY Defendt., the same is continued at ye Plts. cost

p.   Spotsylvania County Court 4th of August 1730
406   - In the action of Trespass upon the Case between WILLIAM STROTHER Gent. Plt.
        and ABRAHAM MAYFIELD & LAZARUS TILLY Defendts. for eight hundred and
thirty nine pounds of tobacco in a hhd. Convenient due p Accot: an Order being confirmed for what should appear due by a Writ of Enquiry against ye said Defendts. and
WILLIAM BECKHAM and JOHN SNELL JUNR. and SAMUEL BROWN their Securities, and a
Jury being sworn to Enquire to the Damage &c., p name LARKIN CHEW &c., who after
having heard all arguements &c. brought in their verdict in these words, Wee of the
Jury find for the Plantiff eight hundred and eighty seven pounds of Tobo: in one hhd:
Convenient damage, LARKIN CHEW, foreman; which Verdict at ye Plts. motion was ad-
mitted to record and Judgment granted for the same with costs & an attorneys fee; It is
therefore ordered that ye sd Defendts. and their securities pay the Plt. the same alias
Exo.
                - Absent GOODRIGHT LIGHTFOOT,
                        WILLIAM HANSFORD, ROBERT GREEN Gentn. Justices
        - In the action of Debt between JONATHAN HOOD, Collier, Plt. and the Honble
ALEXANDER SPOTSWOOD Esqr. Defendt., for two hundred pounds Sterling damage, the
same being agreed, Ordered that the suit be dismist
        - In the action of Debt between WILLIAM STROTHER Plt. and JOHN HEWS Defendt.
a plurias capias is continued
        - In the action of Detinue between GEORGE NIX Plt. and EDWARD PRICE Defendt.
issue joyned for arguement
        - In the action of Debt between OLIVER SEGAR Plt. and ANN JAMES, Admx. &c. of
EDWARD SOUTHALL deced, Defendt., the Defendant put in a Demurrer & time given ye sd
Plt. to consider the same
        - In the action of the Case between JOHN GRAME, Attorney of ye Honble.
ALEXANDER SPOTSWOOD, Plt. and WILLIAM SMALLPEICE Defendt., issue joyned and
referred for tryall
        - In the action of Covenant between WILLIAM SMALPEICE Plt. and JOHN GRAME
Gent. Defendt., the Plt. put in a demurrer and issue and time given ye Defendt to con-
sider the same
        - In the Injunction in Chancery between EDWARD PRICE and GEORGE HOME,
issue joyned for hearing upon Bill, answer and replication
        - In the action of Trespass on the Case between DAVID MITCHELL Plt. and WIL-
LIAM MOORE Defendt. the Plt. moving for Liberty to mend his Declaration was granted
he paying costs; afterwards time given to consider the Defendts. plea & demurrer
                -Absent WILLIAM BLEDSOE, Gent. Justice
        - In the action of Debt between JOHN MORGAN and GRACE his Wife, Admx. of
JOHN HAWKINS deced, Plts. and THOMAS CHEW and LARKIN CHEW, Admrs. &c. of LARKIN
CHEW deced, Defendts., oyer of ye Letters of Administration is granted
                - Present WILLIAM HANSFORD, HENRY GOODLOE, Gent. Justices
                - Absent JOHN SCOTT Gent. Justices
        - In the action of Debt between THOMAS CARR JUNR. Plt. and THOMAS CHEW and
LARKIN CHEW, Admrs. of LARKIN CHEW deced, Defendts., issue joyned for tryall

p.   Spotsylvania County Court 4th of August 1730
407   - In the action of Trespass and Assault between JOHN SCOTT Gent. Plt. and THO-
        MAS CHEW and ROBERT BEVERLEY Gent. Defendts., issue being joyned and put to
a Jury for tryall against THOMAS CHEW p name JOHN TALIAFERRO &c. who after being
sworn and heard all Evedences &c. brought in their Verdict Vizt. Wee of the Jury find

for the Defendant, JOHN TALIAFERRO, foreman; which verdict at the Defendts. motion is admitted to record, And ordered that the Suit be dismist with costs and an attorneys fee; It is therefore ordered that ye sd Plt. do pay the said CHEW the same alias Exo. And the said JOHN SCOTT Plt. put in a replication agst ye sd Defendt. BEVERLEY which ye sd Defendt. joyned for tryall

    - In the action of Trespass upon the Case between WILLIAM BARTLETT and WILLIAM BARTLETT, Assignee of SAMUEL BARTLETT, Plt. and HARRY BEVERLEY Gent. Defendt. for nine hundred and sixty pounds of tobacco due p Accot., The Defendts. demurrer being joyned, the Court having heard all arguements &c. are of oppinion that the said Demurrer is good; Therfore ordered that the Suit be dismist with costs & an attorneys fee; It is therefore considered that ye sd Defendt. recover lagainst ye sd Plantiff his costs and an attorneys fee alias Exo.

    - On the Attachment obtained by CHARLES BARRETT against the Estate of PETER CASSITY which was returned served in the hands of JOSEPH MUTROW, and the said MUTROW came into Court and on Oath declared that he had in his hands Two Shillings & nine pence current money of the sd CASSITYs Estate when ye sd Attachment was served on him, And on motion of ye sd BARRETT ye same is continued

    - In the action of Trespass between WILLIAM HOLLAWAY Plt. and EDWARD PRICE Defendt., issue joyned and referred for tryall

    - In the action of Debt between GEORGE HOME Plt. and WILLIAM RUSSELL Defendt. for Eleven hundred pounds of good Merchantable tobacco in Cask convenient due by Bill; issue being joyned and referred to a Jury for tryall p name JOHN MINOR &c. who after being sworn and heard all Evedences &c. brought in their Verdict in these words Vizt. We of the Jury find for the Plantiff Eleven hundred pounds of Tobacco in Cask convenient according to ye Tenor of the Obligation, JOHN MINOR, foreman, which verdict at the Plts. motion is admitted to record and Judgment granted for the same with costs and an attorneys fee; Afterwards the Defendt. put in an Injunction in Chancery, which was received, (PETER RUSSELL entering himself ye sd Defendts. security in Court to pay the said Debt and Damages if cast)

    - On the Injunction in Chancery exhibitted to Stop proceedings in the action of Trespass upon the Case between THOMAS BENSON and JOSEPH SMITH Gent., the Complt. put in a replication which ye Respondt. joyned issue for hearing upon ye sd Bill, answer and replication next Court

    - In the action of Trespass upon the Case between JOSEPH BROCK Gent., Assee. of WILLIAM SKRINE, Plt., and ANDREW HARRISON, Defendt., special bail being required is rejected, Afterwards Oyer granted

    - In the action of Trespass upon the Case between WILLIAM STROTHER Gent. Plt. and GEORGE HOME Defendt. for three hundred and five pounds of Tobacco convenient due by Note, the said Defendt. came into Court and confessed Judgment for the same with costs and an attorneys fee; It is therefore ordered that the said HOME pay the said STROTHER the same alias Exo.

p.   Spotsylvania County Court 4th of August 1730
408   - In the action of Debt between WILLIAM STROTHER Gent. Plt. and GEORGE HOME Defendt. for twelve hundred and sixty seven pounds of Tobacco in two hhds. in a convenient ROLING HOUSE due by Bill, the said Defendt. came into Court and confessed Jusgment for the same with costs and an attorneys fee; It is therefore ordered that the said Defendt. do pay the Plt. the same alias Exo.

    - In the action of Debt between WILLIAM STROTHER Gent. Plt. and WILLIAM HANSFORD Gent. Defendt., who pleaded payment & issue joyned & referred for tryall

- In the action of Trespass upon the Case between JAMES NICOLL Mercht. and ANDREW HARRISON Defendt., postponed

- In the action of Trespass between JOHN TALIAFERRO JUNR. of CAROLINE COUNTY Gent. Plt. and JOHN GRAME Gent. Defendt., for fifty pounds Sterling damage, the matter of Law arising from the Defendts. Errors in arrest of Judgment being argued, and the Court having heard all arguements on each side are of oppinion that the said Errors are not good; Therefore Judgment is granted for three pounds seven shillings and eight pence Sterling (which was the Jurys verdict) with costs and an attorneys fee; It is therefore ordered that the said GRAME pay the said TALIAFERRO the same alias Exo.

- JOHN FOSTER, Deputy Sheriff, made return of the following Execution Vizt. ALEXANDER McFARLANDs vs the Admrs. of LARKIN CHEW deced, for 1385 lbs Tobo: & 123 lbs. tobo: costs, Executed

- Ordered that the Court be adjourned till to Morrow morning eight of the Clock

- At a Court continued and held for Spotsylvania County August ye 5th: 1730
Present

HENRY WILLIS	WILLIAM BLEDSOE	
WILLIAM HANSFORD	JOSEPH BROCK	Gentlemen Justices

- On the Attachment obtained by Capt. WILLIAM STROTHER against the Estate of EDWARD PRICE for twenty nine hundred and eight pounds of tobacco in three hhds. at Mr. JAEL JOHNSONs ROLING HOUSE, due by Bill, the Sheriff having returned the things attached not sold for want of buyers, On the Plts. motion it is ordered that a Writ of Venditione Exponas do issue

- In the action of Trespass upon the Case between GEORGE MERIDEATH Plt. against WILLIAM SMITH Gent. Defendt., the same is continued

- In the action of Trespass upon the Case between JAMES DYER Plt. and EDWARD WINGFIELD Defendt., order confirmed for what appeared due by Writ of Enquiry next Court

- In the action of Trespass upon the Case between JOHN DAVISON Plt. and PHILIP SANDERS Defendt., for one thousand pounds of tobacco due by account; there being no appearance, Ordered that the same be dismist

p. Spotsylvania County Court 5th of August 1730
409
- In the action of Trespass upon the Case between JOSEPH KEATON Plt. and JOHN SNOW Defendt. Order confirmed agst. ye sd Defendt. & security for what shall appear due p Writ of Enquiry next Court

- In the action of Trespass upon the Case between JOHN SAVAGE Plt. and BENJAMIN WHITE Defendt., for two hundred and twenty pounds of tobacco due p Accot: there being no appearance, Ordered that the said Suit be dismist

- On the Scire facias brought by JOHN SUTTON against HENRY DILLEN and HENRY BERRY, Defendts., the said Defendts. pleaded payment which ye Plt. joyned and referred for tryall next Court

- In the action of Trespass upon the Case between GEORGE HARRISON Plantiff and EDWARD WINGFIELD Defendt. Order confirmed agst. ye sd Defendt. & Sheriff for what shall appear due by Writ of Enquiry next Court

- In the action of Trespass, Assault and battary between JOHN STEVENS Plt. and ABRAHAM BLEDSOE JUNR., Defendt., issue joyned and referred for tryall

- In the action of Debt between EDWARD FRANKLYN Plt. and HENRY CURTIS Defendt., for three hundred pounds of tobacco due by Bill, An order having passed against the said Defendt. and JOHN WIGLESWORTH his security for the non appearance of ye sd Defendt., and he failing now to appear and answer when called, the said Order is confirmed for the same with costs and an attorneys fee; It is therefore ordered that the said Defendt. and his Security do pay the said Plt. the same alias Exo.

- On the Attachment obtained by JAEL JOHNSON, Admx. of RICHARD JOHNSON deced against the Estate of JAMES BOOTH, postponed for an hour

- In the action of Trespass upon the Case between DAVID WAUGH Plt. and THOMAS MALONY Defendt., Order confirmed for what shall appear due by Writ of Enquiry agst. the Defendt. & security next Court

- In the action of Debt between THOMAS CHEW & LARKING CHEW Gent., Admrs. &c. of LARKIN CHEW deced, Plts. and WILLIAM RUSSELL & JAMES McCOLLOUGH Defendts. Order confirmed for what shall appear due p Writ of Enquiry agst. the said Defendt. & security next Court

- In the action of Trespass upon the Case between RICHARD SHARP Plt. and JOHN ELSON Defendt. the alias capias returned not executed, On the Plts. motion a plurias capias is granted

- In the Attachment obtained by JOHN WALLER against the Estate of WILLIAM SMITH Gent., the same is continued

- In the action of Trespass upon the Case between WILLIAM HACKNEY Plt. and JAMES McCULLOGH Defendt., for five pounds twelve Shillings & ten pence current money due by Bill, there being no appearance, Ordered that the same be dismist

- In the action of Trespass upon the Case between ROBERT SPOTSWOOD Plt. and JAMES MORGAIN Defendt., the Defendt. failing to appear and answer, an Order against ye sd Defendt. & security is granted

- In the action of Trespass upon the Case between CHRISTOPHER GRACE Plt. and THOMAS DOWDEY Defendt., at ye sd Defendts. motion oyer is granted him

p.   Spotsylvania County Court 5th of August 1730
410   - In the action of Trespass upon the Case between MARTHA TAYLOR, Executrix of
        the Last Will and Testament of JAMES TAYLOR Gent. deced. Plt. and WILLIAM
RUSSELL Defendt., for four pounds seventeen Shillings current money due by Accot: Mr. JOHN MERCER for and in behalf of the said Defendt. confessed Judgment for the same with costs and an attorneys fee; It is therefore ordered that ye sd Defendt. pay the said Plt. the same alias Exo.

- In the action of Trespass upon the Case between HUGH FRENCH Plt. and BENJAMIN WHITE Defendt., for two pounds Eighteen Shillings and eleven pence current money due by Accot: there being no appearance, Ordered that the suit be dismist

- In the action of Trespass, Assault & Battary between THOMAS ROBINSON Plt. and CHARLES STEVENS & JOHN STEVENS Defendts. for twenty pounds Sterling damage, the Plantiff failing to give security to pay costs if cast when required, Ordered that the Suit be dismist with costs and an attorneys fee; It is therefore ordered that the Plt. pay the said Defendt. their costs & an attorneys fee alias Exo.

- In the Scire facis brought by WILLIAM FLEET against GOODRICH LIGHTFOOT Gent., Late Sheriff, postponed

- In the action of Debt between ROBERT BAYLOR, AUGUSTINE MOORE, WILLIAM TODD & JAMES GARNETT, Exrs. of ye Last Will and Testament of JOHN BAYLOR deced, Plts. and GOODRICH LIGHTFOOT Gent. late Sheriff, Defendt., on the said Defendts. motion, an Imparlance is granted him

- In the action of Debt between JOHN MEALY Plt. and EDWIN HICKMAN Gent. Sheriff of Spotsylvania County Defendt., for two thousand two hundred and twenty five pounds of tobacco and one shilling current money due by Judgment &c., who acknowledged the Declarations and for plea sayd that the said DILLEN broke out of the COUNTY GOAL and made his Escape but suffered Judgment to pass for the same with costs and an attorneys fee; It is therefore ordered that the said HICKMAN do pay the said MEALY the said sum of Two thousand two hundred and twenty five pounds of tobacco and one Shilling current money with costs and an attorneys fee alias Exo.

- In the Scire facias brought by ROBERT BAYLOR against GOODRICH LIGHTFOOT Gent., late Sheriff, the Defendt. put in a demurrer which was joyned & referred for Arguement

- In the action of Debt between JOHN CHAMP Plt. and THOMAS PARKS Defendt., (special bail being required is granted) Order granted agst. ye sd Defendt. and his security

- In the action of Trespass upon the Case between ROBERT THOMAS Plt. and ABRAHAM BLEDSOE JUNR. Order granted agst. the said Defendt. and his security

- In the Scire facias brought by ROBERT BAYLOR, AUGUSTINE MOORE, WILLIAM TODD & JAMES GARNETT, Admrs. of the last Will and Testament of JOHN BAYLOR deced, against GOODRICH LIGHTFOOT, Gent., late Sheriff, the Defendt. put in a demurrer which was joyned and referred for arguement

- Present ROBERT SLAUGHTER Gentleman Justice

p.   Spotsylvania County Court 5th of August 1730
411   - On motion and by consent of JOHN GRAME Gentn. Attorney of the Honble.
ALEXANDER SPOTSWOOD Esqr., and WILLIAM SMALPEICE to have Gentlemen appointed to gage and measure the Carts and the Cole was measured with between them, is granted, and WILLIAM HANSFORD & JOSEPH BROCK Gent. are desired and appointed on Munday before the next Court to meet at the MINES to measure the same and that they have Liberty to Examine Evedences on Oath relating to the premises and what makes a Load of Cole according to Law and Custom and make report of the same to the next Court; And it is further ordered that the Clerk issue summons for what Evedences each party have occasion to make use of to attend at ye time and place aforementioned

- On the petition of EDWIN HICKMAN Gent. Sheriff against HENRY WILLIS Gent. about the non payment of ye Courts order to WM. RUSSELL for fourteen hundred and sixty pounds of tobacco it being agreed, Ordered that the said Petition be dismist

- In the action of the Case between Capt. WILLIAM STROTHER Plt. and PETER CASSADIE Defendt. for three hundred and seventy nine pounds of Tobacco due by Accot: an order being confirmed for what should appear due against ye sd Defendt. and CHARLES BARRATT his security p Writ of Enquiry and a Jury being summoned & sworn to Enquire to the damages &c., p name LARKIN CHEW &c., who after haveing heard all arguements &c. brought in their verdict Vizt. We of the Jury find for the Plt. one pound of tobacco damage, LARKIN CHEW, foreman; which verdict at the Plts. motion was admitted to record and Judgment granted for the same with costs and an attorneys fee; It is therefore ordered that ye sd Defendt. and his Security do pay ye sd Plt. ye same alias Exo.

- On motion of the said Plantiff to have a Minnett taken that the Accot; being mislaid was the occasion of the Jury not finding the said Debt and damages &c. is granted

- In the action of Trespass upon the Case between JAMES NICOLL Plt. and ANDRED HARRISON Defendt., special bail being required is granted, LIkewise ye sd JOHN MERCER assumeing to pay costs and charges if the said Plt. should be cast, the Defendt. afterwards pleaded in Custody & time granted ye Plt. to consider the same

- In the action of Trespass upon the Case between NICHOLAS HAWKINS Plt. and THOMAS BYRN Defendt., for six hundred and forty two pounds of tobacco due by Bill, the same being agreed, ordered that the suit be dismist

- On the Attachment obtained by JAEL JOHNSON, Widow, Admx. of all & singular the goods chattells and Credits of RICHARD JOHNSON deced. against the Estate of JAMES BOOTH for Nine pounds eight shillings & eleven pence Sterling money due by Protested Bill of Exchange &c., Judgment is granted for the same with costs and an attorneys fee and ISAAC MAYFIELD appearing according to Summons and on oath declared that in March Court last the said BOOTH obtained a Judgment against him for Two thousand one hundred and forty six pounds of tobacco with costs; Ordered that the Sheriff do sell the said tobacco p auction as the Law directs for Sterling money for so much thereof as will satisfie the abovesaid debt and costs &c. and make return of his proceedings to the next Court

- On the petition brought by GEORGE BRAXTON Gent. against EDWARD FRANKLYN for two pounds sixteen Shillings & four pence current money due by Bill, the same being agreed, Ordered that ye sd petition be dismist

- On the action of Trespass upon the Case between JOHN CHAMP Plt. and WILLIAM HENSLEY Defendt., for nine hundred pounds of tobacco damage, there being no Declaration filed, or any further prosecution, ordered that ye same be dismist

p.   Spotsylvania County Court 5th of August 1730
412   - On the Attachment obtained by RICHARD PHILLIPS against the Estate of WIL-
LIAM SMITH Gent. for eight hundred thirty seven pounds, eleven shillings and one penny half penny Sterling due as p the Judgment of the Generall Court which is
Vizt: At a Generall Court held at the Capitol October the 28th: 1729
In the action of Debt between WILLIAM CHAMBERLAYNE Plt. and WILLIAM SMITH & RICHARD PHILLIPS Otherwise called We WILLIAM SMITH of St. Georges Parish in the County of Spotsylvania Gent. and RICHARD PHILLIPS of Saint Martins Parish in the County of HANOVER, Planter, Defendts., for eight hundred and thirty seven pounds eleven shillings and one penny half penny Sterling by bond; It is considered that the Plant. recover against the said SMITH and AUGUSTINE SMITH and GOODRICH LIGHTFOOT his Security and against the sd PHILLIPS, BENJAMIN WOODSON and BOOTH NAPIER of GOOCHLAND COUNTY his security the said sum; But this Judgment is to be discharged upon the payment of Four hundred and eighteen pounds fifteen Shillings and six pence three farthing of the Like money, the principall sum mentioned in the condition of the said bond with interest thereupon from the fifteenth day of May One thousand seven hundred and twenty eight till the same is paid and the costs of this Suit and execution is to stay six months: Copy Test JNO. FRANCIS DCGC

for which Judgment is granted with costs and an attorneys fee and the things returned attached Vizt. three Negro men, George, Giles & Poillipus, three Negro women Pat, Nan & Sue, two young Negroes, Phil and Mage; one Scritore Book and papers, 1 corner Cupboard, 4 large framed pictures, 6 small ditto; 1 ovel Table, 1 square ditto; 1 leather chair, 2 chests, 2 small ditto; 4 beds & furniture, three iron potts, 1 iron Spit & Spit Rackes; 2 pair of Iron Pott racks; 2 trunks, 1 set of backgammon Tables, 1 parcell of pewter, 1 large pair of Stilliards & 1 small ditto; 1 pair of scale & Weights & small looking Glass; 1 iron Pessell, 1 Spice Morter & pessell, 1 Bible & other books, 3 parcells of Indian Corn, 1 whip saw, 1/2 barril of 20d nails, 2 small parcills of 8d & 10d ditto; 1 cart & wheels, 1 box iron, and heaters; 4 cows, 1 young bull & 1 calf, and 1 pair of New Cart Wheels; Ordered that the Sheriff do sell the abovesaid things p auction as the Law directs to satisfie and pay the aforementioned Debt and costs and make report of his proceedings to the next Court

- In the action of Trespass upon the Case between MICHAEL GUINNEY Plt. and WILLIAM CARON Defendt., the Defendt. put in a plea & time given the Plt. to consider the same

- In the action of Debt between JOHN SNELL Plt. and JOHN WIGLESWORTH Defendt. for three pounds three shillings current money and ninty seven pounds of Tobo: due by Bill; the same being agreed, Ordered that the Suit be dismist

- In the action of Trespass upon the Case between GEORGE WOODROOFE Plt. and ABRAHAM ABNEY Defendt. for five pounds current money damage, issue being joyned and put to a Jury p name LARKIN CHEW &c., who after being sworn and heard all Evedence &c. brought in their verdict Vizt. We of the Jury find for the Plantiff two pounds thirteen Shillings & six pence Currt. money Damage, LARKIN CHEW, foreman, which verdict at the Plts. motion is admitted to record and Judgment granted for the same with costs and an attorneys fee; It is therefore ordered that the said Defendt. pay the said Plt. the same alias Exo.

- On the Scire facias brought by WILLIAM FLEET Gent. against GOODRICH LIGHT-FOOT Gent., late Sheriff, the Defendt. put in a demurrer which ye Plt. joyned for arguement next Court

- In the action of Trespass upon the Case between JOHN FOSTER, Deputy Sheriff of Spotsylvania County, Plt. and JOSEPH PARKER Defendt., for fifty pounds Sterling damage, & the matter of Law arising from a special verdict being argued and the Court having heard all on each side are of oppinion that the Laws in favour of the Plantiff, Therefore Judgment granted for forty Shillings Sterling which was the Jurys Verdict with costs and an attorneys fee; It is therefore ordered that the Defendant pay the Plt. the same with costs & an attorneys fee alias Exo.

p. Spotsylvania County Court 5th of August 1730
413	- On motion of MARY GAMBRELL, she is allowed for two days attendance and for forty miles comeing and going as she was summoned an Evedence for GEORGE WOODROOFE against ABRAHAM ABNEY; It is therefore ordered that ye sd WOODROOFE pay the said GAMBRELL the same with costs alias Exo.

- ROBERT HUDLESTON is allowed for three days attendance & for thirty three miles comeing and going twice (he having sworn to the time) as he was summoned an evedence for ABRAHAM ABNEY at ye suit of GEORGE WOODROOFE; It is therefore ordered that the said ABNEY pay the said HUDLESTON the same with costs alias Exo.

- In the action of Debt between WILLIAM MORTON Plt. and THOMAS CHEW and LARKIN CHEW, Admrs. with the Will annexed of LARKING CHEW deced, Defendts., the said Defendts. put in a plea and demurrer and time given the Plt. to consider them

- In the action of Debt between the Honble. ALEXANDER SPOTSWOOD Esqr. and THOMAS JARMAN Defendt., the said Defendt. put in a plea and time given the Plt. to consider the same

- On motion of DAVID JONES he having served his Indented time to the Honble. ALEXANDER SPOTSWOOD Esqr. for the Clerk to issue a Certificate and pass for him to Travell &c. the same is granted and ordered that the Clerk do issue the same

- On the Attachment obtained by MARY HAWKINS, Widow, against the Estate of THOMAS TYLER for six hundred pounds of tobacco and fourteen shillings & six pence current money due p Accot: there being no further proceedings, ordered that the same be dismist

- In the action of Trespass upon the Case between THOMAS PHILLIPS Plt. and ADAM HUBARD Defendt., oyer granted the said Defendt.

- In the action of Trespass upon the Case between HENRY JONES Plt. and WILLIAM RUSSELL Defendt., issue joyned and referred for tryall

- EDWIN HICKMAN Gent. Sheriff acquainting this Court that the GOAL and STOCKS are insufficient and out of repair; It is ordered that the said HICKMAN Sheriff do employ some workman to repair the same

- On the Scire facias brought by THOMAS WARE, Ass: of SAMUEL JOHNSON, Plt. against JOHN DAWLEY and JOHN KIMBROW, alias Scire facias is granted

- In the action of Debt between WALTER ANDERSON Plt. and EDWIN HICKMAN Gent. Sheriff, Defendt., special imparlance is granted

- On the petition of MOSLEY BATTALEY against JONAS JENKINGS for Nine hundred and forty four pounds of Tobacco due by Accot:, which the said Plt. proved by Oath, Judgment is granted for the same with costs; It is therefore ordered that the said JENKINS pay the said BATTALEY the same with costs alias Exo.

- On the Scire facias brought by JAMES HORSNAIL Plt. against WILLIAM RUSSELL Defendt., an alias scire facias is granted

- In the action of Trespass upon the Case between RICHARD SHARP Plt. and JACOB WALL Defendt., Order againt ye sd Defendt. in Custody of EDWIN HICKMAN Gent. Sheriff is granted

p.   Spotsylvania County Court 5th of August 1730
414   - In the action of Trespass upon the Case between ALEXANDER GRAVES Plt. and JOHN CONNOR Defendt., an order is granted against ye sd Defendt. & his security

- In the action of Trespass upon the Case between JOHN WALLER Gent. Plt. and EDWIN HICKMAN Gent. Sheriff of Spotsylvania County Defendt., for twelve hundred seven and an half pounds of Tobacco & three hundred & eighty one pounds of Tobo: due by Judgment &c., the same being agreed, ordered that the suit be dismist

- In the action of Trespass upon the Case between WILLIAM FLEET Gent. Plt. and GEORGE HOME Defendt., an alias capias is granted him

- In the action of Trespass upon the Case between JOHN CLAYTON Esqr. Plt. and WILLIAM RUSSELL Defendt. for five pounds & six Shillings & eight pence current money due by a Note &c., Mr. JOHN MERCER for and in behalf of the said Defendt. confessed Judgment for the same with costs & an attorneys fee; It is therefore considered that the said Plt. do recover of the said Defendt. the same with costs and an attorneys fee alias Exo.

- In the action of Detinue between PETER MORRIS Plt. and PATRICK BOLIN, Planter, Defendt. there being no declaration or appearance, ordered that the same be dismist

- JOHN CHEW to make return of the Marks, Weights &c. of the Tobo: tendered & viewed for Mr. AMBROSE MADISON, the same being agreed, ordered that the same be dismist

- On the petition of HENRY WILLIS Gent. about a Road to his MILL in the Fork of the RAPPAHANOCK RIVER, the last Courts order appointing veiwers and the veiwers having not made their return about the same, Ordered that the petition be continued

- On petition of GEORGE HOME, Surveyor of this County, for the delivery of ye County Surveyors Book in the hands of AUGUSTINE SMITH Gent., late Surveyor, ordered that the said SMITH be summoned to answer the same at next Court

- In the Injunction in Chancery to Stop the proceedings of an action of Debt Between JEREMIAH BRONAUGH JUNR. and ROSE his Wife, Admrs. of JOHN DINWIDDIE deced, Plt. and ABRAHAM FIELD, Defendt., the Complainant desired liberty to mend his Bill in Chancery which was rejected, the Court thinking it only to delay the suit, the Complt. put in a replication which was joyned for arguement upon the Bill, answer and replication to the next Court

- In the action of Trespass upon the Case between JOHN SUTTON Plt. and RICHARD LONG Defendt., the same is continued to be tryed the first Jury cause next Court

- JOHN PHILIPS and DINAH his Housekeeper being called to answer the Presentment of the Grand Jury for living in Adultery, it appearing that thay are just married
&c., the same is dismist, the said Philips &c. paying costs
- On the Attachment obtained by JOHN GRAME Gent. Attorney to the Honble.
ALEXANDER SPOTSWOOD Esqr. against the Estate of JAMES JONES for twenty four Shillings current money, the same being no further prosecuted, ordered that he same be
dismist
- In the action of Trespass upon the Case between HENRY CAMPBELL Plt. and
CHRISTOPHER WATERS Defendt., order against ye sd Defendt. and his security is granted

p.   Spotsylvania County Court 5th of August 1730
415   - On the petition brought by ELINOR CRAWLEY against DANIEL BROWN for one
       pound twelve shillings current money due by Bill; And said Defendt. failing to
appear according to summons, Ordered that Judgment be granted for the same with
costs & an attorneys fee: It is therefore ordered that the said Defendt. do pay the said
Plt. the same alias Exo.
- On the action of Debt between THOMAS CHEW Plt. and WILLIAM RUSSELL Defendt., for thirty pounds current money of Virginia due by bond, Mr. ZACHARY LEWIS
for and in behalf of ye sd Defendt. confessed Judgment for seven pounds three Shil-
lings & six pence current money with costs and an attorneys fee: It is therefore
ordered that the said RUSSELL do pay the said CHEW the same alias Exo.
- In the action of Debt between FRANCIS KIRKLEY Plt. and JAMES McCULLOUGH
Defendt., order against Defendt. and Sheriff is granted
- In the action of Debt between JOHN CHAMP Plt. and EDWIN HICKMAN Gent.,
Sheriff, Defendt. a special imparlance is granted
- In the action of Trespass upon the Case between GEORGE YATES Plt. and JOHN
SUTTON Defendt., order against Defendt. & his security is granted
- In the action of Trespass upon the Case between THOMAS LEWIS Plt. and WIL-
LIAM PELLAM Defendt., the same is continued
- In the action of Trespass upon the Case between JOHN FOX Plt. and ANDREW
HARRISON Defendt., order against the Defendant and security
- In the action of Trespass upon the Case between THOMAS CARR JUNR. Plt. and
CHARLES STEVENS Defendt., order against the said Defendant & Sheriff
- In the action of Trespass upon the Case between JOHN STEVENS Plt. and THOMAS
ROBINSON Defendt. for One hundred pounds Sterling, there being no further prose-
cution, ordered that the same be dismist
- In the action of Trespass upon the Case between ABRAHAM LITTLE Plt. and
JAMES CANON Defendt., the same order granted
- In the action of Debt between THOMAS CHEW and LARKIN CHEW, Admrs. with
the Will annext of LARKIN CHEW deced, Plts. and LAZARUS TILLY Defendt., for twenty
pounds Currt. money damage, the same being agreed and no declaration filed, ordered
that the same be dismist
- HARRY BEVERLEY and LARKIN CHEW Gentn. appeared & in Court entered
themselves Special Bail for ANDREW HARRISON at the Suit of JAMES NICOLL, Mercht.
- Ordered that the Court be adjourned to the Court in Course
                                        W. HANSFORD

p.   At a Court held for Spotsylvania County September the first Anno Dom. 1730
416   Present
        GOODRICHLIGHTFOOT   JOSEPH BROCK
        WILLIAM HANSFORD   ROBERT SLAUGHTER
        THOMAS CHEW   WILLIAM JOHNSON   Gentlemen Justices
        HENRY GOODLOE   ABRAHAM FIELD

        - RICHARD BUCKNER Gent. acknowledged his Deeds of Lease and Release for land,
Likewise his Bond for performance of Covenants unto Mr. LAWRENCE BATTAILE at
whose motion the same were admitted to record
        - In the action of Debt between WILLIAM STROTHER Plt. and JOHN HEWS Defendt.,
postponed
        - In the action of Debt between OLIVER SEGAR Plt. and ANN JAMES, Admx. &c. of
EDWARD SOUTHALL deced, Defendt. the said Defendts. demurrer being joyned and referred to the next Court for arguement
        - In the action of Covenant between WILLIAM SMALPEICE &c., Plt. and JOHN
GRAME Gent., Defendt., issue & demurrer joyned and referred for tryall to the next
Court
        - On the Injunction in Chancery brought by EDWARD PRICE Complt. against
GEORGE HOME Defendt., to stay the Judgment obtained by ye sd GEORGE HOME for five
hundred & fifty pounds of tobacco and costs, the Issue being joyned for hearing upon
the sd Bill, answer & replication, the Court having heard all Evedences & arguements
on each side, are of opinion that the Injunction in Chancery is good, and decreed that
the same be made perpetual and the said Suit dismist with costs and an attorneys fee; It
is therefore considered that the ye sd Complt. recover of ye sd Defendt. his costs and an
attorneys fee alias Exo.
        - Present ROBERT GREEN Gent. Justice
        - On petition of JOHN HUFFMAN for to have Liberty to build a CORN MILL & SAW
MILL on the ROBINSON RIVER (he having land on boths sides of ye sd River) near the
GREAT MOUNTAINS, the same is granted
        - JAMES SPARKES acknowledged his Deeds of Lease and Release for land unto
JOHN SCOTT Gent., and JANE SPARKES, Wife of the said JAMES (after being privately
examined) acknowledged her right of dower of the said land unto ye sd SCOTT at whose
motion the same were admitted to be recorded
        - In the action of Trespass upon the Case between DAVID MITCHELL Plt. and
WILLIAM MOORE Defendt.,the Plt. put in a Demurrer & time give ye sd Defendt. to consider the same
        - In the action of Debt between WILLIAM STROTHER Plt. and JOHN HEWS Defendt.,
for eight hundred and five pounds of tobacco due by Bill; Mr. ROBERT GREEN in behalf
of the sd HEWS confessed Judgment for three hundred pounds of Tobo (which was the
ballance) with costs and an attorneys fee; It is therefore ordered that the Defendt. pay
the said Plantiff the same with costs & an attorneys fee alias Execution

p.   Spotsylvania County Court 1st of September 1730
417   - On the Attachment obtained by CHARLES BARRATT against the Estate of PETER
        CASSITY for three hundred and eighty five pounds of Tobo due by Judgment &c.
Judgment is granted for the same with costs and an attorneys fee and JOSEPH MUTROW
having on Oath declared that ahe had two shillings and nine pence current money in
his hands of ye sd CASSITYs Estate, Ordered that the said MUTROW deliver and pay the
said BARRAT the same, and Judgment for the ballance which is three hundred & fifty

seven & a half pounds of tobacco with costs and an attorneys fee; It is therefore ordered that the said CASSITY pay the said BARRATT the same alias Exo.

- In the action of Debt between JOHN MORGAIN & GRACE his Wife, Admx. &c. of JOHN HAWKINS deced, Plts. and THOMAS CHEW & LARKIN CHEW, Admrs. &c. of LARKIN CHEW deced, Defendts. (Mr. LEWIS affirms and agrees that Letters of Administration is granted according to ye order of ESSEX COURT) afterwards the said Defendts. put in a plea, he having liberty to plead divers matters and time given ye sd Plts. to consider the same

- On the Injunction in Chancery obtained by WILLIAM RUSSELL Complt. agst. GEORGE HOME Defendt., the said Defendt. put in a demurrer and time to answer ye same is granted

- In the action of Trespass upon the Case between JOHN SUTTON Plt. and RICHARD LONG Defendt., for one thousand pounds of tobacco cask and conveniency, a Jury being summoned and sworn to Enquire to the damages p name LARKIN CHEW &c. who after having heard all Evedences &c. brought in their verdict Vizt. We of the Jury find for the Plt. One thousand pounds of tobacco in Cask convenient to a Landing and fifteen Shillings current damages, LARKIN CHEW, foreman, which verdict at the Plts. motion was admitted to record and Judgment granted for the same with costs and an attorneys fee; And an Attachment being returned served in the hands of WILLIAM RUSSELL who appeared & declared in Court that he had thirteen hundred and fiveteen pounds of tobacco of the said LONGs in his hands; It is therefore ordered that the said RUSSELL do pay the same unto the said JOHN SUTTON alias Exo.

- In the Injunction in Chancery obtained by JOSEPH SMITH Complt. and THOMAS BENSON Defendt., the same is continued at the said SMITHs costs

- In the action of Trespass upon the Case between JOSEPH BROCK Gent., Assee: of WM. SKRINE, Plt. and ANDREW HARRISON Defendt., ye sd Defendt. put in a pleas which ye Plt. joyned & referred for tryall next Court

- In the Attachment obtained by Capt. WM. STROTHER agst. the Estate of EDWARD PRICE, the Writ of Venditioni Exponas continued

- In the action of Trespass upon the Case between GEORGE MERIDEATH Plt. and WILLIAM SMITH, Gent. Defendt., for two pounds & eleven shillings & six pence current money due by Accot: there being no farther prosecution & being agreed, ordered that ye Suit be dismist

- On the Attachment obtained by JOHN WALLER Plt. agst. ye Estate of WM. SMITH Gent. for nineteen Shillings & ten pence half penny current money & ninety three pounds of tobo; the same order granted

- In the action of Trespass upon the Case between RICHARD SHARP Plt. and JOHN ELSON Defendt., for five hundred & fifty pounds of tobacco due by Accot:, the same order granted

p. 418 Spootsylvania County Court 1st of September 1730

- In the action of Trespass upon the Case between ROBERT SPOTSWOOD Plt. and JAMES MORGAIN Defendt., Order comfirmed for what shall appear due by Writ of Enquiry next Court

- In the action of Trespass upon the Case between CHRISTOPHER GRACE Plt. and THOMAS DOWDEY Defendt., the said Defendt. put in a plea & issue joyned & referred for tryall next Court

- In the action of Debt between ROBERT BAYLOR, AUGUSTINE MOORE, WILLIAM TODD & JAMES GARNETT, Exrs. &c. of JOHN BAYLOR deced, Plts. and GOODRICH LIGHTFOOT Gent., late Sheriff, Defendt., the said Defendt. put in a plea after having Liberty to plead divers matters & time granted the Plts. to consider the same

- Absent GOODRICH LIGHTFOOT, Gent.

- In the Scire facias obtained by ROBERT BAYLOR against GOODRICH LIGHTFOOT Gent. late Sheriff, for three hundred & seventy two pounds of tobacco, the Defendts. demurrer being joyned for argument and the Court having heard all on each side are of opinion that the said Scire facias is good and the said Demurrer not good; Therefore Judgment is granted for the same with costs & an attorneys fee; It is considered that the said BAYLOR recover of the said LIGHTFOOT the same with costs and an attorneys fee alias Execution

- Collo. WILLIAM TODD acknowledged his Deeds of Lease and Release for land unto JOHN SCOTT Gentn. at whose motion the same is admitted to record

- In the action of Trespass upon the Case between GEORGE TILLY, Mercht., Plt. and FRANCIS KIRKLEY Defendt., for three pounds five Shillings & seven pence current money due by Accot: an order being confirmed agst. the said Defendt. & ROBERT SLAUGHTER his Security for what shall appear due p Writ of Enquiry, and the Jury being summoned & sworn by name LARKIN CHEW &c. who after having heard all evedences &c. the next day brought in a Special Verdict Vizt. We of the Jury find that on the Twelve day of April One thousand seven hundred and twenty nine that the said FRANCIS KIRKLEY Defendt. had the goods of the said Plantf. which he is charged with in Accot. produced in Court; We likewise find that the said Defendt. was by agreemt. to lett the sd Plantiff have a quantity of Tobo: wch the sd Defendt. failed to comply with; We likewise find that the said Defendt. did Lend to ye Plantiff one pound seven shillings and two pence in the hands of ROBERT SLAUGHTER which the said Plantiff did refuse; We likewise find that the said Plantiff did fail to gitt the goods for the said Defendt. according to there agreemt.; We likewise find for the Plant. one pound fifteen Shillings current money damage if the Law be for him if not we find for the Defendt. LARKIN CHEW, foreman; which was ordered to be recorded and referred to the next Court for argument

- GEORGE PENN acknowledged his Deeds of Lease and Release for land unto DAVID WILLIAMS and JAMES COWARD in behalf of the said DAVID desired the same might be admitted to record which was granted

- On the petition of GEORGE HOME, Surveyor, for the Delivery of the County Surveyors Book in the hands of AUGUSTINE SMITH Gent., late Surveyor, the said SMITH came into Court and affirmed that he never had or ever kept a pertcular Book for that purpose p reason the County would never purchase a Book, Ordered that the said Petition be dismist

- In the action of Debt between JOHN CHAMP Plt. and THOMAS PARKS Defendt., for four thousand & thirty seven pounds of Right good sound well handled tobacco in five hhds. & clear of cask due by Bill; An order having last Court past against the sd Defendt. & JOHN BOND his security for the non appearance of the said Defendt., & he now failing to appear when called this, the said order is confirmed for the same with costs & an attorneys fee; It is therefore ordered that the Defendt. and JOHN BOND his security do pay the said Plt. the same alias Exo.

p.
419
Spotsylvania County Court 1st of September 1730

- In the action of Trespass upon the Case between ROBERT THOMAS Plt. and ABRAHAM BLEDSOE JUNR. Defendt. for six hundred and sixty three pounds of Tobo: due by Accot: special bail being required was granted. Mr. ABRAHAM BLEDSOE SENR. came into Court and entered himself special bail for the Defendt. who afterwards confessed Judgment for the same with costs & an attorneys fee; It is therefore ordered that the said Defendt. pay the said Plt. the same alias Exo.

- On the Scire facias brought by ROBERT BAYLOR, AUGUSTINE MOORE, WILLIAM TODD & JAMES GARNETT, Exrs. &c. of JOHN BAYLOR Deced, against GOODRICH LIGHTFOOT Gent., late Sheriff, continued at the Defents. costs for him to produce his Books

- In the action of Trespass upon the Case between JAMES NICOLL, Mercht., Plt. and ANDREW HARRISON Defendt., continued at the Plts. costs

- In the Attachment obtained by JAEL JOHNSON, Admx. &c. of RICHD. JOHNSON deced agst. ye Estate of JAMES BOOTH, the Sheriff having returned the Court order for outcry, ordered that ye same be dismist

- On the Attachment obtained by RICHARD PHILIPS against the Estate of WILLIAM SMITH on the said Plts. motion the former Judgment is made Voyde & ordered that the same be dismist

- In the action of Trespass upon the Case between MICHAEL GUINNEY Plt. and WILLIAM CARON Defendt., the Plt. put in a demurrer and time granted ye sd Defendt. to consider the same

- On the Scire facias brought by WILLIAM FLEET Gent. agst. GOODRICH LIGHTFOOT Gent., late Sheriff, continued at the Defendts. costs for him to produce his Books

- In the action of Debt between WILLIAM ORTON Plt. and THOMAS CHEW & LARKIN CHEW, Admrs. &c. of LARKIN CHEW deced, Defendts. issue joyned & referred to next Court for tryall

- In the action of Debt between the Honble. ALEXANDER SPOTSWOOD Esqr. Plt. and THOMAS JARMAN Defendt., the said Plt. put in a replication & time given ye sd Defendt. to consider the same

- In the action of Trespass upon the Case between THOMAS PHILIPS Plt. and ADAM HUBBARD Defendt., further Oyer granted

- On the Scire facias brought by THOMAS WARE, Ass: of SAMUEL JOHNSON, against JOHN DAWLEY & JOHN KIMBROW for three pounds Eleven Shillings & five pence current money, & three hundred & eighteen pounds of Tobo: due by Judgment &c., Judgment is renewed for the same with costs & an attorneys fee; It is therefore ordered that the said DAWLEY & KIMBROW pay ye sd Plantiff the said sum of three pounds Eleven Shillings & five pence current money and three hundred & eighteen pounds of tobo. with costs & an attorneys fee alias Exo.

- In the action of Debt between WALTER ANDERSON PLt. and EDWIN HICKMAN, Gent. Sheriff, Defendt., the said Defendt. put in a plea & time given ye sd Plt. to consider the same

- On the Scire facias brought by JAMES HORSNAIL Plt. agst. WILLIAM RUSSELL Defendt., (Mr. ZACHARY LEWIS entered himself Security for ye sd Plt., he being out of the Country, to pay costs if cast) afterwards ye sd Defendt. pleaded which was joyned & referred for tryall to next Court

p. 420 Spotsylvania County Court 1st of September 1730

- In the action of Trespass upon the Case between RICHARD SHARP Plt. and JACOB WALL Defendt., for one thousand nine hundred and twenty six pounds of tobacco due by Note & Accot:, the said Defendt. came into Court and confessed Judgment in Custody of EDWIN HICKMAN Gent. Sheriff for the same with costs & an attorneys fee; It is therefore ordered that the said Defendt. in Custody as aforesaid pay ye Plt. the same alias Execution

- In the action of Trespass upon the Case between ALEXANDER GRAVES Plt. and JOHN CONNER Defendt., for three pounds fifteen shillings current money due by Note; (special bail being granted). And an order having passed last Court agst ye sd Defendt. and ALEXANDER HOWARD his security for the non appearance of ye sd Defendt., and he now failing to appear when called and answer the suit, order is confirmed for the same with costs & an attorneys fee; It is therefore ordered that the sd Defendt. and his security pay ye sd Plt. the said sum of three pounds fifteen shillings current money with costs and an attorneys fee alias Execution

- In the action of Debt between WILLIAM FLEET Gent. Plt. and GEORGE HOME Defendt., special bail being required is granted, Likewise Oyer granted

- On the petition of Collo. HENRY WILLIS to have a Road to his MILL in the Fork of RAPPAHANOCK RIVER from Mr. JOHN FINLESONs ROAD to the upper Inhabitants and from the said Road to his Mill &c., the veiwers appointed having made their report, On the said WILLIS's motion an order is granted for a review and ordered that Mr. FRANCIS SLAUGHTER, FRANCIS KIRKLEY & WILLIAM PAYTON do view the same and that the Surveyor of that part of the County with the aforesaid three Gentlemen do lay of ye same the most nighest & convenient way (att the said WILLIS's Charge) and make report of their proceedings to the next Court

- In the action of Debt between JEREMIAH BRONAUGH JUNR. & ROSE his Wife, Admx. of JOHN DINWIDDIE deced, Plts. and ABRAHAM FIELD Defendt. the same is postponed till tomorrow morning

- Ordered that the Court be adjourned till to Morrow morning Nine of the Clock

- At a Court continued & held for Spotsylvania County September the Second Anno Dom 1730   Present
            WILLIAM HANSFORD   JOSEPH BROCK
            THOMAS CHEW   ABRAM FIELD   Gentlemen Justices

- In the action of Trespass upon the Case between HENRY CAMPBELL Plt. and CHRISTOPHER WATERS Defendt., An order confirmed for what shall appear due by Writ of Enquiry next Court

- In the action of Debt between FRANCIS KIRKLEY Plt. and JAMES McCULLOUGH Defendt., special bail being granted, Mr. ROBT. SPOTSWOOD came into Court and entered himself special bail for ye sd Defendt., afterwards ye sd Defendt. put in a plea & time is given ye sd Plt. to consider the same

- In the action of Debt between JOHN CHAMP Plt. and EDWIN HICKMAN Gent. Sheriff Defendt., ye sd Defendt. put in a plea & time given the Plt. to consider the same

p.   Spotsylvania County Court 2d of September 1730
421   - In the action of Trespass upon the Case between GEORGE YATES Plt. and JOHN
        SUTTON Defendt., Order confirmed for what shall appear due p Writ of Enquiry
next Court

- In the action of Trespass upon the Case between THOMAS LEWIS Plt. and WILLIAM PELLAM Defendt., the same is continued

- In the action of Tresspon upon the Case between JOHN FOX Plt. and ANDREW HARRISON Defendt., Judgment by Nihil Dicit is granted

- In the action of Trespass upon the Case between THOMAS CARR JUNR. Plt. and CHARLES STEVENS Defendt., the said Defendt. pleaded which the Plt. joyned and tryall thereof is referred to next Court

- Absent ABRAM. FIELD Gent. Justice

- Ordered that the County Levy be laid next Court & that the Sheriff do give Publick Notice accordingly

- Present WILLIAM JOHNSON
          ROBERT GREEN   Gentlemen Justices

- Ordered that JOHN HOLLADAY, JOHN KEY, ROBERT KING and JOHN WIGLES-
WORTH or any three of them whereof the said JOHN WIGLESWORTH shall be one (being
first sworn before a Magestrate of this County) do value the Timber made use of in
building a BRIDGE over the RIVER PO in MINE ROAD and unto whom ye said Timber did
belong to and make report of their proceedings to the next Court
          - Present JOHN SCOTT, Gentleman Justice
     - In the action of Debt between JEREMIAH BRONAUGH JUNR. & ROSE his Wife,
Exrs. &c. of JOHN DINWIDDIE deced, Plts. and ABRAHAM FIELD Defendt., the same is continued at the Plts. costs till the same shall be called again
     - Ordered that the Sheriff do send a Messenger to the Clerk of the Assembly for a
Certificate of this County Cridit for Woulves Heads & about the IRON MINE Exempted
Tithables &c. against the laying of the County and Parish levy
     - On motion of HENRY McKEY, he is allowed for two days attendance as he was
summoned an evedence for JEREMIAH BRONAUGH JUNR. & ROSE his Wife, Admrs. of
JOHN DINWIDDIE Gent. deced, and for thirty eight miles comeing and going and for
forages at ye WIDOW JOHNSONs (he having sworn to the time) It is therefore ordered
that the said BRONAUGH &c. do pay the said McKEY the same alias Exo.
     - JOHN COBURN thesame order granted for Thirty six miles vs. Ditto
          - Present HENRY WILLIS Gent. Justice
               GOODRICH LIGHTFOOT Gentn.
     - In the action of Debt between SAMUEL SKINKER Plt. and GEORGE HOME Defendt.
oyer granted

p.   Spotsylvania County Court 2d of September 1730
422   - In the action of Detinue between GEORGE NIX Plt. and EDWARD PRICE Defendt.,
     for Twenty pounds Sterling damage, issue being joyned and referred to a Jury
for tryall p name JOHN WHEELER &c., who after being sworn and heard all evedences
&c. brought in their verdict Vizt. We of the Jury find for the Plantiff One pounds fifteen shillings Sterling for the Mare and five shillings Sterling for the Bell, JOHN
WHEELER, foreman, which verdict at the Pts. motion was admitted to record and the
Matter of Law being then argued the Court were of opinion that the same was in favour
of ye Plt., Therefore Judgment is granted for the same with costs & an attorneys fee; It
is therefore ordered that the said Defendt. pay the said Plt. the same alias Exo.
     - In the action of Trespass upon the Case between JOHN & MARY CHANDLER, Exrs.
of ANDREW LEITCH deced, Plts. and MICHAEL ONEAL Defendt., for seven hundred & fifty
pounds of Tobo: &c. by Note, the same being agreed, Ordered that the suit be dismist
     - On the Scire facias brought by JOHN BLOWERS against JOHN PARKS for twenty
four pounds of Tobo: & fifteen Shillings current money or One hundred and fifty
pounds of Tobo: due by Judgment &c., Judgment is renewed for the same with costs & an
attorneys fee; It is therefore ordered that the said PARKS do pay the said BLOWERS the
same alias Execution
     - In the action of Trespass upon the Case between ABRAHAM LITTLE Plt. and
JAMES CANON Defendt., for three pounds three shillings current money due by Accot;
the same being agreed, ordered that the suit be dismist
     - In the action of Trespass upon the Case between JAMES PHILIPS Plt. and ADAM
STRAUGHN Defendt., for fifty Shillings current money due by Accot: no further prosecution, ordered that the same be dismist
     - In the action of Trespass upon the Case between ABRAHAM ABNEY Plt. and
GEORGE WOODROOFE Defendt. for one hundred pounds current money damage, the said
Plt. failing to appear and prosecute the said suit, On the Defendts. motion an nonsuit

with costs & an attorneys fee is gratned him; It is therefore ordered that ye said Plt. pay ye sd Defendt. the same alias Exo.

- In the action of Trespass upon the Case between JOHN BUCKNER Plt. and AN-DREW HARRISON Defendt, a special Imparlance is granted

- On the Scire facias brought by JOHN BUCKNER against ANDREW HARRISON Defendt., the said Defendt. demurred generally which ye sd Plt. joyned and referred for arguement next Court

- On the Attachment obtained by JOHN WALLER against the Estate of JOHN MEALY for three hundred & fifty thre & a half pounds of tobo: due for Clerkes Fees as p Accot; which the said Plt. made out on Oath to be due. Therefore Judgment is granted for the same with costs and the Attachment being returned served on the Tobo: in the hands of EDWIN HICKMAN Gent. Sheriff; It is therefore ordered that the said Sheriff do deliver & pay the said WALLER ye abovesaid Judgment & costs out of ye said tobacco of ye sd Defendts. in his hands as the aforesaid Defendant recovered against the sd HICKMAN Sheriff for two thousand two hundred & twenty five pounds of tobacco and one Shilling currant money and costs August ye 5th: 1730

- On the Attachment obtained by ZACHARY LEWIS against the Estate of JOHN MEALY for nine hundred and thirty eight pounds of tobacco due by Accot: which ye sd Plt. made out on Oath; Therefore Judgment is granted for the same with costs and the Attachment being returned served on the tobacco in the hands of EDWIN HICKMAN Gentn. Sheriff; It is therefore ordered that the said Sheriff do deliver and pay the said LEWIS ye abovementioned sum of nine hundred & thirty eight pounds of tobacco with costs out of the said Tobacco of the said MEALYs in his hands as the sd Defendt. recovered against ye said HICKMAN Sheriff for two thousand two hundred & twenty five pounds of tobacco and one shilling currant money

p.   Spotsylvania County Court 2d of September 1730
423   with costs & in Spotsylvania Court August ye 5th: 1730

- On the Attachment obtained by JOHN GORDEN against the Estate of JOHN MEALY for Nine hundred and ten pounds of tobacco which the said Plt. made out on Oath to be due; therefore Judgment is granted him for the same with costs and an attorneys fee; And the Attachment being returned served on the tobacco in the hands of EDWIN HICKMAN Gentn. Sheriff (as the said Defendant recovered Judgment against the said Sheriff for two thousand two hundred & twenty five pounds of tobacco & one Shilling currant money damages with costs & in Spotsylvania County Court August the fifth 1730) It is therefore ordered that the said Sheriff do deliver & pay unto the said Plantife the above said sum of Nine hundred and ten pounds of tobacco with costs & an attorneys fee out of the said Tobacco of the sd MEALYs Defendt. in his hands, or so much thereof as remain in his hands after JOHN WALLERs & ZACHARY LEWIS Judgments with costs as they have obtained agst. the sd Defendants Estate and first paid & satisfied

- In the action of Trespass upon the Case brought p RICHARD LONG & JOHN FOX Plts. against ANDREW HARRISON Defendt., (special bail being required is granted) afterwards on the Defendants non appearance, an order passed against him & GEORGE WOODROFE his security

- In the action of Trespass upon the Case brought p THOMAS CLAYBOURN Plt. against GEORGE HOME Defendt., who failing to appear when called, on the Plts. motion an order is granted against the said Defendant & EDWIN HICKMAN Gent. Sheriff

- In the action of the Case brought p JOHN GRAME Gent., Attorney of the Honble. ALEXANDER SPOTSWOOD Esqr., Plt. against WILLIAM SMALLPEICE Defendt., the same is continued at the Defendts. costs & untill ye said action be called againe for his Attorney to bring his Books &c.

- On the motion of THOMAS ELSON, he is allowed for two days attendance as he was summoned an evedence for GEORGE NIX vs. EDWARD PRICE; It is therefore ordered that the said NIX do pay the said ELSON the same alias Exo.

- In the action of Debt brought p THOMAS CARR JUNR. Plt. against THOMAS CHEW & LARKIN CHEW, Admrs. with the Will annext &c. of LARKIN CHEW deced, Defendts. the same is continued at the Defendants costs

- In the action of Trespass & Assault brought p JOHN SCOTT Gentn. against THOMAS CHEW and ROBERT BEVERLEY Gentn. the said BEVERLEY haveing pleaded seperately which was joyned p the Plantife & put to a Jury for tryall p name GEORGE TILLY &c.,who after being sworn &c. brought in their verdict Vizt. Wee of the Jury find for the Plantife Forty Shillings Sterlin Damage, JOHN WHEELER, foreman, afterwards the Plea of Abatement and the Errors moved in arrest of Judgment being argued were over ruled p the Court; Therefore on ye Plantifes motion the said verdict was admitted to record & Judgment granted for the same with costs & an attorneys fee, It is therefore ordered that the said BEVERLEY do pay the said SCOTT the same alias Exo.

- ROBERT TURNER, Deputy Sheriff, made returne of ALEXANDER SPOTSWOODs Esqr. Exo. vs. THOMAS DAVIS for ten pounds nine shillings & five pence & five hundred & sixty nine pounds of tobacco costs; not Executed

- In the action of Trespass upon the Case brought p JAMES DYER Plt. against EDWARD WINGFIELD Defendt. for seven pounds currant money damage; Judgment having passed last Court for what shall appear due p Writt of Enquiry this, and the Jury being sworn p name GEORGE HOME &c. who having heard all evedences and arguements brought in their Verdict Vizt. Wee of the Jury find for the Plantife (the remainder of this page has been torn off)

p.   Spotlsylvania County Court 2d of September 1730
424   - On motion of Capt. THOMAS CHEW, he is allowed for three days attendance as he
        was summoned an evedence for ROBERT BEVERLEY Gentn. vs JOHN SCOTT Gentn.
It is therefore ordered that the said BEVERLEY do pay the said CHEW the same alias Exo.

On motion of LARKIN CHEW, he is allowed for three days attendance as he was summoned an Evedence for ROBERT BEVERLEY Gentn. vs. JOHN SCOTT Gentn. It is therefore ordered that the said BEVERLEY do pay unto the said CHEW the same alias Exo.

- On motion of JOHN MINOR he is allowed for two days attendance as he was summoned an Evedence for JOHN SCOTT Gentn. vs ROBERT BEVERLEY Gentn. It is therefore ordered that the said SCOTT do pay the said MINOR the same alias Exo.

- On motion of JAMES COWARD, he is allowed for two days attendance as he was summoned an Evedence for JOHN SCOTT Gent. vs ROBERT BEVERLEY Gentn., It is therefore ordered that the said SCOTT do pay the said COWARD the same alias Exo.

- Capt. THOMAS LCHEW & Capt. WILLIAM JOHNSON came into Court and entered themselves special bail for ANDREW HARRISON at the suit of JOHN FOX.

- GOODRICH LIGHTFOOT, WILLIAM BLEDSOE & ABRAHAM FIELD Gentn. or any two of them are appointed & desired p the Court & impowered to agree with workmen to mend and repair the COUNTY PRISON and make returne of their proceedings to ye next Court

- WILLIAM MOORE came into Court and entered himself a special bail for GEORGE HOME at the suit of WILLIAM FLEET Gentn.

- Ordered that the Court be adjourned till ye Court in Course
                                        G. LIGHTFOOT

- At a Court held for Spotsylvania County on Tuesday October the Sixth: 1730

Present

GOODRICHLIGHTFOOT	ROBERT SLAUGHTER	
JOHN TALIAFERRO	ABRAM FIELD	Gentlemen Justices
WILLIAM BLEDSOE	ROBERT GREEN	

- JOHN COLLIER JUNR. acknowledged his Deed with Livery & Seizen for Land unto ROBERT STUBLEFEILD & ANN, the Wife of the said JOHN, Power of Attorney to JOHN WALLER Gent. being first proved p the oath of ROBERT DUDLEY, the said WALLER acknowledged her right of Dower of ye Land unto the said STUBLEFIELD at whose motion the same was admitted to record

- ROBERT STUBLEFIELD acknowledged his Deed for Land unto JOHN COLLIER JUNR. at whose motion the same was admitted to record

- WILLIAM BLEDSOE Gent. acknowledged his Deeds of Lease and Release for Land unto JOHN TALIAFERRO Gentn. at whose motion the same was admitted to be recorded

- Present HENRY WILLIS Gent.

- In the action of Trespass between WILLIAM HOLLAWAY Plt. and EDWARD PRICE Defendt. for five pounds Sterling damage, issue being joyned and put to a Jury for tryall p name ANDREW HARRISON &c. who after being sworn & heard all evedence &c. brought in their verdit in these words, We of the Jury find for the Defendant, ANDREW HARRISON, foreman, which verdict at the Defents. motion was admitted to record and ordered that the Suit be dismist with costs & an attorneys fee; It is therefore ordered that the said Plt. do pay the said Defendt. the same alias Exo.

p.   Spotsylvania County Court 6th of October 1730
425   - Absent HENRY WILLIS, Gent.

- AUGUSTINE SMITH Gent. acknowledged his Deeds of Lease and Release for land unto WILLIAM FANTLEROY and at the motion of JOHN TALIAFERRO Gent. in behalf of the said FANTLEROY the same was admitted to be recorded

- GEORGE CARR & CORDELIA CARR bond for performance of Covenants to BENJAMIN BERRYMAN for the conveying of a Lot of Land in FREDERICKSBURGH TOWN was proved p the Oaths of HENRY WILLIS, THOMAS HILL Gentn. and at the motion of JOHN TALIAFERRO Gent. in behalf of ye sd BERRYMAN the same was admitted to record

-Present HENRY WILLIS, Gent.

- JOHN COOK acknowledged his Deeds of Lease and Release for land unto WILLIAM BOHANNAN, and ANN COOK, wife of the said JOHN (after being privately examined) acknowledged her right of Dower of the said Land unto the said BOHANAN at whose motion the same was admitted to record

- HENRY FOX's Deed with the Livery & Seizen for land unto SAMUEL HENDERSON was proved p the Oaths of WILLIAM JONES, JOHN MALLARY & NIGHTINGALL DALBY and at the said HENDERSONs motion the same was admitted to record

- Present WILLIAM HANSFORD & JOHN SCOTT Gent.

- JOHN ASHLEY acknowledged his Deeds of Lease & Release for land unto WILLIAM SMITH, and MARY ASHLEY, Wife of the said JOHN (after being privately examined) acknowledged her right of Dower of the said Land unto the said SMITH, at whose motion the same was admitted to record

- ROWLAND THOMAS acknowledged his Deeds of Lease & Release for Land unto ROBERT TURNER at whose motion the same were admitted to record

- On petition of THOMAS JACKSON to have his buildings works & Improvements &c. valued by two or more men upon Oath as the Law directs with regard to Account of

Expences that he have been at in Seating a certain tract of land laying in this County is granted & ordered that BENJAMIN CAVE, DAVID PHILIPS, WILLIAM PHILIPS & JOHN HARSUIPE or any three of them being first sworn before a Magestrate of this County, do value the several kind of buildings and Improvements and on what part of the said Land they are, and make report of their proceedings to the next Court

p.   Spotsylvania County Court 6th of October 1730
426   - Present THOMAS CHEW Gent.
  - In the action of Debt between WILLIAM STROTHER Gent. Plt. and WILLIAM HANSFORD Gent. Defendt., for ten pounds Sterling damage, issue being joyned and put to a Jury for tryall p name LARKIN CHEW &c., who after being sworn & heard all Evedence &c. brought in their verdict in these words; We of the Jury find for the Plantiff Six pence Sterling damage, LARKIN CHEW, foreman; which verdict at the Plts. motion was admitted to record and Judgment granted for the same with costs & an attorneys fee; It is therefore ordered that the said Defendt. pay the said Plt. the same alias Exo.
  - JOHN CHAMBERS, Deputy Sheriff of STAFFORD County, made returne of WM. RUSSELLs Exo. vs JOHN BLACKLEY for ₤ 5...8... and 404 lbs. of Tobo. costs. Not Executed
  - On motion of JAMES ROY, he is allowed for three days attendance as he was summoned an Evedence for EDWARD PRICE at the suit of WILLIAM HOLLOWAY (he having sworn to the time) It is therefore ordered that the said PRICE pay the said ROY the same alias Exo.
  - On motion of JOHN GRAYSON JUNR. he is allowed for three days attendances as he was summoned an Evedence for WILLIAM HOLLAWAY against EDWARD PRICE (he having sworn to the time); It is therefore ordered that the said HOLLAWAY pay the said GRAYSON the same alias Exo.
  - In the action of Trespass upon the Case between JOSEPH KEATON Plt. and JOHN SNOW Defendt., for two pounds current money due by Accot: the suit being agreed, Ordered that the same be dismist
  - On the Scire facias brought by JOHN SUTTON Plt. against HENRY DILLEN & HENRY BERRY Defendts., for one thousand two hundred and fifty pounds and a quarter of Tobo: & three hundred and twenty four pounds of Tobo: costs due by Judgment &c., issue being joyned and put to a Jury for trayll p name GEORGE PROCTER &c., who after being sworn & heard all evedences &c. brought in their Verdict Vizt. We of the Jury find for the Defendant, JOHN STEVENS, foreman; which verdict at the said Defendts. motion was admitted to record and Ordered that the same be dismist with costs and an attorneys fee; It is therefore ordered that the said SUTTOn pay the said Defendt. the same alias Exo.
  - PHILIP BRANEGON acknowledged his Deeds of Lease and Release for land unto JOHN WELLS at whose motion the same was admitted to record
  - EDWIN HICKMAN Gent. Sheriff made return of JOHN FOSTERs Exo. vs. JOSEPH PARKER for ₤ 210...0 Sterlin and 895 1/2 lbs Tobo: costs; Executed
  - GEORGE DUGLASS is allowed for three days attendance as he was summoned an Evedence for HENRY DILLEN & HENRY BERRY at the Suit of JOHN SUTTON (he having sworn to the time) & for fifty miles comeing & going twice; It is therefore ordered that the said DILLEN & BERRY pay the said DUGLASS the same alias Exo.
  - WILLIAM DENN the same order granted
  - On motion of Mr. WILLIAM RUSSELL he is allowed for one days attendance for Ditto ads. Ditto
  - JOHN FOSTER, Deputy Sheriff, made return of the following Exo.s Vizt.
JOHN BLOWERS vs JOHN PARKS for 24 lbs. Tobo: & 15 Currt. & 258 lbs. Tobo. Costs, Exe-

cuted; ELINOR CRAWLEY vs. DANLL. BROWN for L 1...12... Currt. money & 255 lbs. Tobo: costs, Executed

p.   Spotsylvania County Court 6th of October 1730
427   - On motion of HENRY BERRY to have Liberty to withdraw ROBERT HOLMS Bill &
         Recepts. made use of & produced in the Suit between JOHN SUTTON and HENRY
DILLEN & HENRY BERRY for fourteen hundred pounds of tobacco, the same is granted
after the same is recorded which are Vizt.

    This Bill shall obleadg me ye Subscriber me my heirs Executor
and Administrators to pay unto HENRY DILLEN he his heirs &c. ye full
and Just sum of Fourteen hundred pounds of good sound sweet sented
Tobacco in two Casks & caske being all ready by a greivance & ye one
hhd. to be paid Ready down paid and hhd. on ye tenth of October next
insueing ye date hereof in Witness hereof I have hereunto set my hand
this 28th: of Febry: 1727/8.

        ROBERT   his mark   HOLMS

Test WM. TERRELL
     THOS.LIGHTFOOT
March ye 5: 1727/8
    Then Reced of Mr. ROBT. HOLMS seven hundred pounds of Toba:
being in part of the within Bill
        Reced pr. JOHN SUTTON

Janry: 8 day 1728
    Then Reced of ROBT. HOLMS full sattisfaction for the within Bill
Reced p JOHN SUTTON

- On motion of THOMAS HILL, he is allowed for three days attendance as he was
summoned as an evedence for WILLIAM HANSFORD Gent. at the suit of WILLIAM
STROTHER gent. (he having sworn to the time) It is therefore ordered that the said
HANSFORD pay the said HILL the same alias Exo.

- On motion of CHARLES GOODALL, he is allowed for One day attendance as he was
summoned an evedence for JOHN SUTTON vs. HENRY DILLEN & HENRY BERRY, & for
forty two miles comeing and going; It is therefore ordered that ye sd SUTTOn pay the
said GOODALL the same alias Exo.

- THOMAS CHEW & LARKIN CHEW acknowledged their Deeds of Lease & Release to
CHARLES CHISWELL Gent. which at the motion of JOHN WALLER JUNR. in behalf of the
said CHISWELL the same was admitted to record

- On motion of GEORGE PROCTER, he is allowed for three days attenance as he was
summoned an evedence for WILLIAM HOLLAWAY agst. EDWARD PRICE (he having
sworn to the time). It is therefore ordered that the said HOLLOWAY pay the said PROCTER
the same alias Exo.

- On petition of WILLIAM FRAZIER for administration of DAVID MITCHELL deced
Estate (he being the greatest Creditor as appears) is granted, and he having taken the
oath and entered into bond with JOHN GORDEN & JAMES ROY his securitys and acknowledged the same in Court, Ordered that Certificate be granted ye sd FRAZIER for
obtaining Letters of Administration in due form, And that PHILEMON CAVENAUGH,
JAMES WILLIAMS, URIAH GARTON & JAMES GARTON or any three of them (being first
sworn before a Majestrate of this County) do some time between this & the next Court
appraise such of the said DAVID MITCHEL deced Estate as shall be produced & shewn
them p the sd Administrator and make report of their proceedings to the next Court

- Ordered that the Court be adjourned till to Morrow moring at nine of the Clock

p.   <u>At a Court continued & held for Spotsylvania County Octoberthe Seventh Anno</u>
428 <u>Dom: 1730</u>   Present
                   HENRY WILLIS   JOHN SCOTT
                   JOHN TALIAFERRO   ABRAHAM FIELD   Gentlemen Justices
                   ROBERT SLAUGHTER   ROBERT GREEN

       - Ordered tha the Sheriff do summons a Grand Jury to attend the next Court as
the Law directs
       - HENRY WILLIS & JOHN WALLER Gent., two of the Trustees of FREDERICKSBURGH
TOWN acknowledged their Deed for a Lot of Land numbered 51 unto JOHN WILLIAMS
Gent. and at the motion of JOHN MERCER in behalf of the said WILLIAMS the same was
admitted to record
       - Then the Court proceeded to Lay the County Levy, Vizt.
                   Spotsylvania County is   Dr.

Mens Names	Wolves Heads	p whom granted	Tobacco
ROBERT GREEN Ass: of JOHN HEWS	2	p ABRAM. FIELD Gentn.	400
JOHN TALIAFERRO Asse. of THOS. DOWNER	1	p JOHN TALIAFERRO	200
DITTO Ass: of HENRY HAWS	1	Ditto	200
ABRAM FIELD Ass: of RICHD. JENKINGS	1	p ABRAM FIELD	200
DITTO Ass. of JAMES MORGAIN	1	p. ROBERT GREEN	200
RICHARD BARNES Ass: of JOHN HEWS	1	p Ditto	200
Ditto Ass: of JOHN AXFORD	3	p ROBERT SLAUGHTER	600
JOHN SCOTT, Ass: TIMOTHY DALTON	1	p JOHN SCOTT	200
DENNIS LINDSEY	1	p ROBERT GREEN	200
PATRICK GRADEY	3	p ROBERT SLAUGHTER	600
Ditto Ass: of JOHN PAYTON	3	p Ditto	600
JOHN SKELTON	2	p HENRY WILLIS	400
ROBERT TURNER, Ass: of JOHN SHAW	1	p ROBERT GREEN	200
ELISHA PERKINS	7	p ROBERT SLAUGHTER	1400
Ditto	3	Ditto	600
EDWIN HICKMAN, Ass. of GEO: MUSICK	4	p THOMAS CHEW	800
Ditto Ass. of THOS ALLEN	4	p Ditto	800
NICHOLAS YEAGER	1	p ABRAM FIELD	200
CHRISTOPHER ZIMMERMAN Ass. JACOB CRIGLER	1	p Ditto	200
Ditto Ass. of ELISHA PERKINS	1	p ROBERT SLAUGHTER	200
JACOB CRIGLER	1	p Ditto	200
JOSEPH HAWKINS, Ass. of JOHN MOORE	1	p JOHN SCOTT	200
Ditto	1	p Ditto	200
GOODRICH LIGHTFOOT	7	p ROBERT SLAUGHTER	1400
JOHN TURRELL	1	p JOHN SCOTT	200
WALTER BUTLER	1	p ROBERT GREEN	200
JOHN DURRETT	1	p JOSEPH BROCK	200
CHARLES HUTCHESON	1	p WILLIAM JOHNSON	200
BENJAMIN CAVE	4	p WILLIAM BLEDSOE	800
JOSEPH WILLIAMS	1	p HENRY WILLIS	200
Ditto	1	p Ditto	200
JAMES ROY	1	p AMBROSE GRAYSON	200
WILLIAM WALLER	1	p THOMAS CHEW	200
FRANCIS TUNLEY	1	p AMBROSE GRAYSON	200
	65		13000

p.   <u>Spotsylvania County Court 7th of October 1730</u>

429	To brought over 65 Amounting to	13000
To Majr. JOHN TALIAFERRO for a Coroners Fee of a Saylor		133
To Ditto for Ditto of PETER WATSON		133
To Ditto for Ditto of JOHN STRAUGHN		133
To Ditto for Ditto of JOHN PURVIS JUNR.		133
To THOMAS COLLAHAN for Sumoning a Jury of Inquest for JOHN STRAUGHN & JOHN PURVIS JUNR.		100
To HENRY HERRINGTON for Ditto for the Sailor		50
To ALEXANDER McQUEEN for ditto for PETER WATSON		50
To PAUL MICO for 3: County Levys overcharged		73 1/2
To Widow ELIZABETH TALIAFERRO for 4 Levys Overcharged, paid by WILLIAM PHILIPS		110
To SAMUEL BALL for 1 Ditto last year		27 1/2
To JOHN KILGORE for 1 Ditto		24 1/2
To EDWIN HICKMAN Sheriff for 19 Delinquents @ 24 1/2 p Poll		405 1/2
To the Secretary for Secretarys fees omitted last year		50
To Mr. ZACHARY LEWIS as Kings Deputy Attorney with Cask as p Accot.		1296
To JOHN WALLER Clerk his yearly Sallary as p Law		1080
To EDWIN HICKMAN Gent. Sherif his yearly Sallary as p Law		1080
To JOHN GORDEN for keeping Prisoners, mending ye Prison, Candles, Small Beer &c., as per Accot:		1510
To Mr. GEORGE HOME Surveyor for a County Surveying Book		400
To JOHN WALLER Clerk for Record Book & Copy Laws as p Accot:		4100
To EDWIN HICKMAN Sheriff for sending down to Wmsburg. for the Laws &c.		500
To Mr. ROBERT SPOTSWOOD for keeping the FERRY at GERMANNA		2000
To Mr. CHARLES CHISWELL for paid JOHN WIGLESWORTH for makeing the BRIDGE over the RIVER PO		3000
To Cask & Conveniencey 18 p Cent of do		540
		26991
To Sallary to the Sheriff for Collecting 26991 Tobo. at 10 p Cent		2699

CREDITOR

By the Courts Order to EDWIN HICKMAN Gent. Sheriff on Colo. HENRY WILLIS for the Ballance of the Countys Tobacco that was proportioned p the Assembly Anno. 1728 & Lodged in his hand	6266		
By the Courts order to JOHN WALLER on HARRY BEVERLEY Gent. for L 3...10...4 being the ballance of the Countys Tobacco (as he sold which was proportioned p the Assembly Anno. 1728 in part of the said WALLERs County Claim	703		
	6969	6969	
		22721	

The whole County Charge amounting unto Twenty two thousand seven hundred and twenty one pounds of Tobacco to be levied on Fourteen hundred & sixty five Tithables Comes to fifteen and a half pounds of tobacco p Poll (and fourteen pounds of tobacco the fraction will be due to the Sheriff) Which EDWIN HICKMAN Gent. Sheriff is ordered and impowered to collect & receive the same from those to whom the said Tithables or any of them do belong; and pay and satisfie the respective County Creditors (he having entered into Bond with GOODRICH LIGHTFOOT and ABRAHAM FIELD Gent. his securitys as the Law directs) And in case of non payment he is impowered to levy the same by distress

- HARRY BEVERLEY Gent. is ordered & desired to pay unto JOHN WALLER or his order three pounds ten shillings & four pence current money (as he accepts of in part of his County Claim) it being the ballacne due from him to the County on Accot: of the tobacco's that was proportioned p the Assembly Anno. 1726 in MIDLESEX & ESSEX Countys (as he sold & accounts with the Court for in August Court 1728:) & this shall be his discharge for the same

p.   Spotsylvania County Court 7th of October 1730
430   - HENRY WILLIS Gent. is ordered & desired to pay unto EDWIN HICKMAN Gent.
Sheriff for order six thousand two hundred & sixty six pounds of tobacco, it being the ballance due the County Tobacco that was proportioned p the Assembly Anno 1728 in KING & QUEEN, GLOCESTER, MIDLESEX, LANCASTER & NORTHUMBERLAND Countys and was Lodged in his hands
- Then the Court adjourned for half an hour

- At a Court continued & held p Adjournment for Spotsylvania County October the 7th 1730   Present

HENRY WILLIS	ROBERT SLAUGHTER
GOODRICH LIGHTFOOT	JOHN SCOTT
JOHN TALIAFERRO	ABRAHAM FIELD Gentlemen Justices
THOMAS CHEW	ROBERT GREEN

- On motion of GEORGE HOME he is allowed for three days attendance as he was summoned an Evedence for WILLIAM HOLLAWAY against EDWARD PRICE (he having sworn to the time); It is therefore ordered that the said HOLLAWAY do pay the said HOME the same alias Exo.
- Twenty six thousand seven hundred one & a half pounds of Tobacco being due & proportioned by the last Assembly for this County, Colo. HENRY WILLIS is ordered to receive the same of the several Countys where the same be proportioned & that the Clerk do issue orders on the several Sheriffs for the same, the said WILLIS agreeing & promising the Court to pay the same quantety in this County next year (the EASTERN SHORE Tobacco excepted); and the Tobacco he is desired to sell for the best advantage he can for the Countys use & to be answerable to the County for the same when demanded
- It is agreed p this Court to give & allow Colo. ALEXANDER SPOTSWOOD Esqr. three thousand pounds of Tobacco to have the FERRY at GERMANNA well kept for this Ensueing year
- Colo. HENRY WILLIS is ordered & desired to procure & gett the printed Laws for each Justice (as was made the last Assembly) and that the County do repay him again the same
- Ordered that DANIEL BROWN, RICHARD BLANTON, WILLIAM BARTLETT & JOHN WIGLESWORTH or any three of them (being first sworn before a Majestrate of this County) do value the Timber made use of in building a BRIDGE over the RIVER PO in the MINE ROAD in tobacco and unto whom the Timber did belong to and make return of their proceedings to the next Court
- HENRY WILLIS & JOHN TALIAFERRO Gent. are appointed to Employ & agree with any Workman to mend and repair the COUNTY GOAL & make report of their proceedings to the next Court
- Ordered that the Court be adjourned till the Court in Court
HEN: WILLIS

(Being our Part IV and concluding part of Spotsylvania County Order Book 1724-1730)

ABBOTT. Roger 62.

ABNEY. Abraham 16, 28, 45, 60, 61, 63, 72, 80; Dennit Jr. 27.

ALLEN. Thomas 5, 11, 21, 35, 43, 45, 53, 54, 55, 86; William 9.

ALLING. Thomas 26.

ANDERSON. George 41; Walter 26, 34, 36, 32, 73, 78.

ANDREWS. Robert 14.

ARNOLD. Francis 16, 28, 38.

ASHER. John 30, 51.

ASHLEY. John 47, 83; Mary 83.

ASHTON. Birdine 3.

ASKUE. John 42.

AXFORD. John 86.

BAGG. Edmund 9, 24; John 27, (Revd.-30).

BAINS. William 45.

BAKER. Thomas 43.

BALDWIN. Warren 12.

BALL. Samuel 23, 87.

BARNES. Robert 86.

BARON. William (a Servant boy -62).

BARRETT. Charles 44, 64, 67, 70, 75.

BARTLETT. Samuel 2, 17, 36, 55, 67; William 2, 13, 17, 30, 33, 36, 42, 43, 46, 50, 55, 67, 88.

BATTALEY. Lawrence 75; Mosley 1, 28, 51, 52, 73.

BAYLOR. John 69, 70, 76, 78; Robert 5, 69, 70, 76, 77, 78.

BEAL. Thomas 4.

BECKHAM (BICKHAM). William 7, 10, 23, 34, 51, 54, 56, 63, 64, 66.

BELL. William 14.

BENSON. Thomas 3, 4, 7, 8, 17, 18, 20, 29, 37, 45, 56, 67, 76.

BERNARD. Michael 14; Robert 61.

BERRY. Henry 14, 58, 68, 84, 85.

BERRYMAN. Benjamin 47, 83.

BEVERLEY. Harry 2, 7, 17, 22, 24, 26, 38, 42, 44, 55, 67, 74, 87, 88; Robert 42, 59, 66, 82; William 18 (of Essex Co.-51).

BICKERS. Robert 42, 43, 47; William 15.

BLACKLEY. John 4, 21, 23, 84.

BLANTON. Margaret 40; Richard 27, 40, 42, 43, 46, 50, 51, 62, 88; William 40.

BLEDSOE. Abraham Junr. 38, 57, 58, 68, 70, 77; Abraham Senr. 77; Isaac 22; William 3, 14, 15, 21, 82, 83, 96.

BLOODWORTH. Joseph (Petition to prove right to take up land -22), 39; Mary 22.

BLOWERS. John 80, 84.

BOHANNAN. William 83.

BOLDING. Patrick 30, 73.

BOND. John 28, 29, 31, 46, 51, 77.

BOOTH. James 10, 32, 41, 44, 52, 58, 69, 71.

BOURN. Robert 13.

BOWMAR. John 40.

BRADBOURN. Sarah 30; William 30.

BRANCH: Walnut 9.

BRANEGON. Philip 84.

BRAXTON. George 2, 71.

BRAY. David 49.

BRIDGE: County 1; East North East 1, 16; Mine 62; over River Ny 13, 14, 33, 64; over River Po 13, 19, 80, 87, 88; Wallers 1; Wilderness Run 15, 33, 50.

BROCK. Joseph 3, 15, 19, 30, 38, 53, 56, 60, 67, 70, 76, 86.

BRONAUGH. Jeremiah Jr. 2, 3, 17, 32, 46, 63, 73, 79, 80; Rose 2, 3, 17, 32, 46, 63, 73, 79, 80.

BROWN(E). Daniel 7, 15, 33, 74, 85, 88; Samuel 66; William 33, 39.

BRYANT. Richard 1.

BUCKNER. John 81; Richard 75.

BURGES(S). Charles 10, 25, 34.

BUSH. John 42, 43, 46.

BUTLER. Walter 51, 86.

BYRN (BURN). Thomas 3, 4, 11, 20, 71.

CAMMELL. Henry 10; John 35, 59, 64.

CAMPBELL. Henry 74, 79; John 3.

CANNEY. James 23; James Jr. 9.

CANNON. James 17, 21, 37, 74, 80; Mary 17; William 57.

CARDER. John 8, 24, 26, 39.

CARON. William 72, 78.

CARR. Cordelia 47, 83; George 47, 83; Thomas 15; Thomas Junr. 17, 27, 28, 36, 35, 66, 74, 79, 82.

CARTER. Mr. Secretary 14.

CARTERET. Honble. Edward 65.

CASSADIE (CASSITY)(CUSTODIE). Peter 44, 57, 60, 64, 67, 70, 75.

CAVE. Benjamin 2, 8, 9, 15, 42, 84, 86; David 31, 65; Robert 65.

CAVENAUGH. Charles 13, 33, 47; Philemon 1, 2, 13, 33, 40, 43, 47, 85.

CHAMBERLAYNE. William 71.

CHAMBERS. John (Dep. Sheriff of Stafford Co.-23), 84.

CHAMP(E). John 28, 36, 64, 70, 71, 74, 77, 79.

CHANDLER. John 80; Mary 80.

CHAPMAN. John 40.

CHEEK. Jane 30; Richard 7, 12, 23, 26, 27, 30, 32, 35, 37, 54, 55, 58, 59, 61.

CHEW. John 8, 11, 43, 44, 45, 59, 63, 73; Larkin 2, 3, 5, 8, 9, 15, 16, 17, 25, 31, 36, 38, 42, 46, 47, 48, 53, 55, 59, 60, 61, 65, 66, 68, 69, 70, 72, 74, 77, 78, 82, 84, 85; Thomas 2, 5, 8, 15, 16, 17, 25, 31, 36, 42, 47, 48, 53, 55, 59, 60, 61, 66, 69, 72, 74, 78, 82, 85, 86.

CHISWELL. Charles 4, 8, 12, 13, 18, 19, 46, 49, 58, 62, 85, 87.

CHRISTOPHER. John 15, 51; Nicholas 1, 6, 11.

CHURCH. Mattapony 5, 46; Pay for a Glebe 52; South West Mountain Chappell 9.

CLAYBOURNE. Nathaniel (Surveyor-61); Thomas 81.

CLAYTON. John 73.

CLINCH. Barbary (Servant -18).

CLOWDER. Jeremiah 5, 37, 50, 55.

COBURN. John 80.

COLLAHAN. Thomas 87.

COLLEY. George 11, 14, 63.

COLLIER. Ann 83; John Jr. 83.

CONNOR. John 73, 78.

CONNYERS. Henry 28.

CONWAY. Francis 1.

COOK. Ann 12, 83; Daniel 65; John 12, 31, 83; Michael 15, 42; Thomas 31.

COOPER. Barbary 62; Joseph 11, 25, 62.

COPLAND. Nicholas 14.

CORNELIUS. Richard 28, 37.

COTTMAN. Benjamin 22; Joseph 17.

COUNTY: Levy 14, 15, 86, 87; Goal 31, 36, 43, 51, 73, 88; Prison 7, 60, 82; Caroline 17, 30, 31, 33, 51; Essex 30, 51, 88; Gloster 88; Goochland 71; Hanover 31, 55, 71; King George 1, 9, 63; King & Queen 88; Lancaster 88; Middlesex 88; Northumberland 88; Prince George 31; Stafford 51; Westmoreland 3.

COURT HOUSE Road to 2.

COWARD. James 41, 42, 77, 82.

CRAWFORD. William 14.

CRAWLEY. Elinor 74, 85.

CREDERS (CRETHERS). Thomas 5, 46, 50, 55, 57.

CRIGLER. Jacob 86.

CRIME & PUNISHMENT: Not assisting Deputy Sheriff 3; Breaking out of Prison 3, 7, 70; Swear Oaths 15, 16, 52, 64; Not frequenting Parish Church 16, 28, 29; Breach of Sabbath by suffering wagons & Cattle to be drove 16, 28, 37; Having a bastard Child 47; Living in Adultery 52, 64, 74; Drunk in Court 60; Breaking the Stocks 60, 63.

CUDDIN(G) John 57; William 4, 8, 57.

CURTIS. Charles 5; Henry 52, 58, 64, 68; Rice 42, 43, 47, 49, 50, 64; Rice Junr. 12, 26, 41.

DALBY. Nightingall 83.

DALTON. Timothy 86.

DAVIS. Thomas 5, 6, 21, 29, 53, 82; William 2.

DAVISON. John 57, 68.

DAWLEY. John 28, 73, 78.

DENN. William 84.

DILLEN 70; Henry 58, 68, 84, 85.

DINWIDDIE. John 2, 3, 17, 32, 46, 63, 73, 79, 80.

DONOLSON. Andrew 16, 29.

DOWDEY. George 11, 33; John 2, 18, 29; Thomas 14, 38, 69, 76.

DOWNER. Thos. 86.

DUDLEY. Robert (Dep. Sheriff of Caroline Co.-61), 83.

DUETT. Charles Junr. 10, 26, 27, 34, 54, 65; John 22, 25, 26, 34, 54.

DOUGLASS. George 84.

DUNCOMB. William 62.

DURRETT. John 46, 51, 86.

DYER. James 7, 57, 68, 82.

EDDINS. Wm. 13, 15.

ELLIOTT. John 3.

ELLIS. Robert 16, 29.

ELSON. John 57, 58, 69, 76; Thomas 82.

EVANS (EVENS). Robert 26, 27, 28, 34, 36, 52, 64

FANTLEROY. William 83.

FERRY. At Fredericksburg 22, 48; At Germanna 14, 37, 87, 88; Johnson's over Rappahannock River 42.

FIELD. Abraham 2, 3, 14, 17, 32, 41, 46, 73, 79, 80, 82, 86, 87; Henry 1, 51, 52.

FINALSON. John 46, 47, 48, 60, 63, 79.

Heritage Books by Ruth and Sam Sparacio

Abstracts of Account Books of Edward Dixon,
Merchant of Port Royal, Virginia, Volume I: 1743–1747

Abstracts of Account Books of Edward Dixon,
Merchant of Port Royal, Virginia, Volume II

Albemarle County, Virginia Deed and Will Book Abstracts, 1748–1752

Albemarle County, Virginia Deed Book Abstracts, 1758–1761

Albemarle County, Virginia Deed Book Abstracts, 1761–1764

Albemarle County, Virginia Deed Book Abstracts, 1764–1768

Albemarle County, Virginia Deed Book Abstracts, 1768–1770

Albemarle County, Virginia Deed Book Abstracts, 1771–1772

Albemarle County, Virginia Deed Book Abstracts, 1772–1776

Albemarle County, Virginia Deed Book Abstracts, 1776–1778

Albemarle County, Virginia Deed Book Abstracts, 1778–1780

Albemarle County, Virginia Deed Book Abstracts, 1780–1783

Albemarle County, Virginia Deed Book Abstracts, 1783–1785

Albemarle County, Virginia Deed Book Abstracts, 1785–1787

Albemarle County, Virginia Deed Book Abstracts, 1787–1790

Albemarle County, Virginia Deed Book Abstracts, 1790–1791

Albemarle County, Virginia Deed Book Abstracts, 1791–1793

Albemarle County, Virginia Deed Book Abstracts, 1793–1794

Albemarle County, Virginia Deed Book Abstracts, 1794–1795

Albemarle County, Virginia Deed Book Abstracts, 1795–1796

Albemarle County, Virginia Deed Book Abstracts, 1796–1797

Albemarle County, Virginia Will Book Abstracts:
1752–1756 and 1775–1783

Albemarle County, Virginia Will Book: 2, 1752–1764

Albemarle County, Virginia Wills, 1764–1775

Albemarle County, Virginia Will Book: 3, 1785–1798

Augusta County, Virginia Land Tax Books, 1782–1788

Augusta County, Virginia Land Tax Books, 1788–1790

Amherst County, Virginia Land Tax Books, 1789–1791

Caroline County, Virginia Appeals and Land Causes, 1787–1794

Caroline County, Virginia Appeals and Land Causes, 1795–1800

Caroline County, Virginia Committee of Safety and Early Surveys,
1729–1762 and 1774–1775

Caroline County, Virginia Guardian Bonds 1806–1821

Caroline County, Virginia Land Tax Book Alterations, 1782–1789

Caroline County, Virginia Land Tax Book Alterations, 1789–1792

Caroline County, Virginia Land Tax Book Alterations, 1792–1795

Caroline County, Virginia Land Tax Book Alterations, 1795–1798

Caroline County, Virginia Order Book Abstracts, 1765

Caroline County, Virginia Order Book Abstracts, 1767–1768

Caroline County, Virginia Order Book Abstracts, 1768–1770

Caroline County, Virginia Order Book Abstracts, 1770–1771

Caroline County, Virginia Order Book, 1764

Caroline County, Virginia Order Book, 1765–1767

Caroline County, Virginia Order Book, 1771–1772

Caroline County, Virginia Order Book, 1772–1773

Caroline County, Virginia Order Book, 1773

Caroline County, Virginia Order Book, 1773–1774

Caroline County, Virginia Order Book, 1774–1778

Caroline County, Virginia Order Book, 1778–1781

Caroline County, Virginia Order Book, 1781–1783

Caroline County, Virginia Order Book, 1783–1784

Caroline County, Virginia Order Book, 1784–1785

Caroline County, Virginia Order Book, 1785–1786

Caroline County, Virginia Order Book, 1786–1787

Caroline County, Virginia Order Book, 1787, Part 1

Caroline County, Virginia Order Book, 1787, Part 2

Caroline County, Virginia Order Book, 1787–1788

Caroline County, Virginia Order Book, 1788

Culpeper County, Virginia Deed Book Abstracts, 1769–1773

Culpeper County, Virginia Deed Book Abstracts, 1778–1779

Culpeper County, Virginia Deed Book Abstracts, 1781–1783

Culpeper County, Virginia Deed Book Abstracts, 1785–1786

Culpeper County, Virginia Deed Book Abstracts, 1788–1789

Culpeper County, Virginia Deed Book Abstracts, 1791–1792

Culpeper County, Virginia Deed Book Abstracts, 1795–1796

Culpeper County, Virginia Land Tax Book, 1782–1786

Culpeper County, Virginia Land Tax Book, 1787–1789

Culpeper County, Virginia Minute Book, 1763–1764

Digest of Family Relationships, 1650–1692,
from Virginia County Court Records

Digest of Family Relationships, 1720–1750,
from Virginia County Court Records

Digest of Family Relationships, 1750–1763,
from Virginia County Court Records

Digest of Family Relationships, 1764–1775,
from Virginia County Court Records

Essex County, Virginia Deed and Will Abstracts, 1695–1697

Essex County, Virginia Deed and Will Abstracts, 1697–1699

Essex County, Virginia Deed and Will Abstracts, 1699–1701

Essex County, Virginia Deed and Will Abstracts, 1701–1703

Essex County, Virginia Deed and Will Book, 1692–1693

Essex County, Virginia Deed and Will Book, 1693–1694

Essex County, Virginia Deed and Will Book, 1694–1695

Essex County, Virginia Deed and Will Book, 1695–1697

Essex County, Virginia Deed and Will Book, 1697–1699

Essex County, Virginia Deed and Will Book, 1701–1704

Essex County, Virginia Deed and Will Book, 1745–1749

Essex County, Virginia Deed, 1753–1754 and Will Book 1750

Essex County, Virginia Deed Abstracts, 1721–1724

Essex County, Virginia Deed Book, 1724–1728

Essex County, Virginia Deed Book, 1728–1733

Essex County, Virginia Deed Book, 1733–1738

Essex County, Virginia Deed Book, 1738–1742

Essex County, Virginia Deed Book, 1742–1745

Essex County, Virginia Deed Abstracts, 1745–1749

Essex County, Virginia Deed Book, 1749–1751

Essex County, Virginia Deed Book, 1751–1753

Essex County, Virginia Land Trials Abstracts, 1711–1741

Essex County, Virginia Order Book Abstracts, 1695–1699

Essex County, Virginia Order Book Abstracts, 1699–1702

Essex County, Virginia Order Book Abstracts, 1716–1723, Part 1

Essex County, Virginia Order Book Abstracts, 1716–1723, Part 2

Essex County, Virginia Order Book Abstracts, 1716–1723, Part 3

Essex County, Virginia Order Book Abstracts, 1716–1723, Part 4

Essex County, Virginia Order Book Abstracts, 1723–1725, Part 1

Essex County, Virginia Order Book Abstracts, 1723–1725, Part 2

Essex County, Virginia Order Book Abstracts, 1725–1729, Part 1

Essex County, Virginia Order Book Abstracts, 1727–1729, Part 2

Essex County, Virginia Order Book, 1695–1699

Essex County, Virginia Will Abstracts, 1730–1735

Essex County, Virginia Will Abstracts, 1735–1743

Stafford County, Virginia Deed Book, 1722–1728 and 1755–1765
Stafford County, Virginia Land Tax Books, 1782–1792
Stafford County, Virginia Order Book, 1664–1668 and 1689–1690
Stafford County, Virginia Order Book, 1691–1692
Stafford County, Virginia Order Book, 1692–1693
Stafford County, Virginia Will Book, 1729–1748
Stafford County, Virginia Will Book, 1748–1767
Westmoreland County, Virginia Deed and Will Abstracts, 1723–1726
Westmoreland County, Virginia Deed and Will Abstracts, 1726–1729
Westmoreland County, Virginia Deed and Will Abstracts, 1729–1732
Westmoreland County, Virginia Deed and Will Abstracts, 1732–1734
Westmoreland County, Virginia Deed and Will Abstracts, 1734–1736
Westmoreland County, Virginia Deed and Will Abstracts, 1736–1740
Westmoreland County, Virginia Deed and Will Abstracts, 1740–1742
Westmoreland County, Virginia Deed and Will Abstracts, 1742–1745
Westmoreland County, Virginia Deed and Will Abstracts, 1745–1747
Westmoreland County, Virginia Deed and Will Abstracts, 1747–1748
Westmoreland County, Virginia Deed and Will Abstracts, 1749–1751
Westmoreland County, Virginia Deed and Will Abstracts, 1751–1754
Westmoreland County, Virginia Deed and Will Abstracts, 1754–1756
Westmoreland County, Virginia Order Book, 1705–1707
Westmoreland County, Virginia Order Book, 1707–1709
Westmoreland County, Virginia Order Book, 1709–1712
Westmoreland County, Virginia Order Book, 1712–1714
Westmoreland County, Virginia Order Book, 1714–1716
Westmoreland County, Virginia Order Book, 1716–1718
Westmoreland County, Virginia Order Book, 1718–1721

www.ingramcontent.com/pod-product-compliance
Lightning Source LLC
Chambersburg PA
CBHW080338270326
41927CB00014B/3272